Not too Late

of related interest

The Psychology of Ageing
An Introduction 2nd edition
Ian Stuart-Hamilton
ISBN 1 85302 233 0

Shakespeare as Prompter
The Amending Imagination and the Therapeutic Process
Murray Cox and Alice Theilgaard
ISBN 1 85302 159 8

Structuring the Therapeutic Process
Compromise with Chaos: The Therapist's Response to the Individual and the Group
Murray Cox
ISBN 1 85302 028 1

The Listening Reader
Fiction and Poetry for Counsellors and Psychotherapists
Ben Knights
ISBN 1 85302 266 7

Grief and Powerlessness
Helping People Regain Control of their Lives
Ruth Bright
ISBN 1 85302 386 8

What Do You See?
Phenomenology of Therapeutic Art Expression
Mala Betensky
ISBN 1 85302 261 6

Music for Life
Aspects of Creative Music Therapy with Adult Clients
Gary Ansdell
ISBN 1 85302 299 3 pb
ISBN 1 85302 300 0 CD

Discovering the Self through Drama and Movement
The Sesame Approach
Edited by Jenny Pearson
ISBN 1 85302 384 1

Music Therapy Research and Practice in Medicine
From Out of the Silence
David Aldridge
ISBN 1 85302 296 9

Not too Late
Psychotherapy and Ageing

Ann Orbach

Foreword by Joseph Redfearn

Jessica Kingsley Publishers
London and Bristol, Pennsylvania

First published in the United Kingdom in 1996 by
Jessica Kingsley Publishers Ltd
116 Pentonville Road
London N1 9JB, England
and
1900 Frost Road, Suite 101
Bristol, PA 19007, U S A

Copyright © 1996 Ann Orbach

Foreword Copyright © 1996 Joseph Redfearn

Library of Congress Cataloging in Publication Data
A CIP catalogue record for this book is available from the Library of Congress

British Library Cataloguing in Publication Data
Orbach, Ann
Not too late : psychotherapy and ageing
1. Psychotherapy for the aged
I. Title
618.9'768914

ISBN 1-85302-380-9

Printed and Bound in Great Britain by
Athenaeum Press, Gateshead, Tyne and Wear

'Tis not too late to seek a newer world.

Alfred, Lord Tennyson, *Ulysses*

Acknowledgements

My special thanks to Janet Aldridge for her thoughtful reading and constructive criticism of my manuscript, and to Elizabeth Reisz, who, with great patience, taught me the rudiments of word processing and printed my text on her computer. I would also like to thank the many friends and colleagues whose encouragement made this book possible and, most of all, those patients, old and young, who generously allowed me to write about them.

Contents

Foreword

Twenty-five years ago I remember a much respected, not-yet-elderly Jungian analyst, one of the awesome few who 'had known Jung personally', saying that in every analyst's practice there would eventually be one or two patients with whom she/he would 'walk together into the sunset'. Most of us present at that conference took that as an amusing way of admitting that analysts have failures, but now, after practising in the same locality for many decades, I feel quite differently. In the first place, the fact that some stay in therapy longer than others makes it inevitable that long-term patients will predominate more and more as one gets older oneself, and that the average age of one's patients will steadily increase. In the second place, I find that remaining in therapy a long time may more often than not mean that one is getting a lot out of it, so that long-term is not synonymous with unsuccessful. In this book, Ann Orbach shows how satisfying working with the elderly patient or as an elderly therapist can be.

In Western and other populations people are living longer and having fewer children. If we continue to retire at the same age, say, 65, and thereupon cease to be economically productive, the economic burden on the young of us pensioners, whether we are drawing state pensions or living off hard-earned savings, may become a major social stress unless those elderly people who remain able to work are encouraged to do so. Much more flexible, less 'ageist', attitudes may therefore become necessary and may actually come into being, unless mass unemployment threatens the young and causes them to continue to squeeze out the elderly in the scramble for jobs. The fact that the elderly will continue to have voting power, which will become more and more important as time goes on, will of course exercise politicians, more, perhaps, than it should. So, with all these sociological factors at work, we should foresee the danger of the 'us' and 'them' gap or barrier between young and old increasing and adding to the other destructive us/them divides of this world.

The result of successful therapy, in the individual, is the achievement of more communication across these barriers inside the patient her/himself. That between the parent and the child in oneself is of course of all-pervading importance in the therapy of young and old alike, and affects many other boundaries in us, for example the good person and the bad person boundary, and that between male and the female, and between the motherly and the fatherly subpersonalities in each of us. The effects of therapy spreads beyond the individual. The intrapsychic and the social divides act and react one upon the other. But how therapeutic therapists and therapists' ideas can be for society as a whole is of course a moot point.

To my mind this book helps wonderfully towards diminishing the hostile or dismissive 'us' and 'them' as between the younger person and the older person both intrapsychically and interpersonally. Ann does not instruct us on how to conduct therapy on 'them', i.e. old people. Instead, we are given a view across the boundary, first from one side, then from the other, before being gently helped to explore the world of the old person in ourselves, and eventually to accompany the older person on her journey in the final chapters on ending, on the ageing therapist, and on matters of life and death. It is all 'us' rather than 'them', and this takes away some of the terror which tends to possess us when we see decrepitude and dissolution only from across an abyss.

The message in this book, which is also its title, is conveyed by the companionship of its author and her attentiveness and respect for her patients, whose dignity is not merely allowed to be preserved, but if anything enhanced. I vividly remember, when a few years ago it was thought that I might well have cancer, someone urging me to take a 'positive-thinking' attitude and a leap of faith and thus 'cure myself'. I may be quite atypical, but I felt I would rather die than behave in such a false and undignified way. It was the first time that I had ever thought about dignity in relation to myself, and it is certainly not of any great concern to me in the normal run of my life. But it is extremely easy to feel patronized when one is vulnerable and in the throes of rethinking one's identity and future.

Even to old people, or especially to old people perhaps, the word 'old' is a 'them' not 'me' word. How many of us old people feel like an old person? All right, except on bad days perhaps. One may look a bit bent; one may have various aches and pains; one is disinclined to walk so far (mind you, one could if really necessary!); one cannot hear low frequencies or remember names so well; more and more one finds that one has heard all the news and views before. But one still feels no different as far as being 'young' or 'old' is concerned. One simply feels oneself – age doesn't really come into it. In dreams the same is true – others often are of a particular age but not so often oneself. In the transference, and in relation to important others, one may feel like a baby, a lover, a sister, a mother or father – perhaps as one gets older one's repertoire of roles and feelings expands if anything. The truism 'You are as old as you feel' is of course strictly nonsense – you feel as old as you feel and you are as young as you feel. But to feel old, old being such a 'them' word, is to feel superfluous and cast out. Actually *being* cast out, even if only to the extent of being patronized by whippersnappers, may be the last straw. One needs to be allowed to rethink one's identity at one's own pace, so as to remain one of 'us'.

I think people nowadays are much kinder to each other – kinder to children, animals, women (or men), blacks (or white, etc.), old people, non-co-religionists, and other 'thems', than they were, give or take some horrifying backlashes. In the work of bridge-building between the different parts of ourselves, therapy lies at one end of the scale, persecution of 'enemies' at the other, with sequestration, a sometimes necessary evil, in-between. It is fairly easy for most therapists to remain comfortably identified with their patient for an hour every week, whereas longer or more frequent sessions might be a strain, or maddening, or even physically damaging to the therapist in terms of wear and tear. It is others who make the greater sacrifices, or who erect their own appropriate defences.

But this is certainly not an argument against therapy. As we know from experience, an hour a week can make all the difference about how one sees oneself, how one feels about oneself, how one re-invents oneself, and how one 'fits in with the arrangements'. Reading this book, both as a therapist and an old man, has made me feel a lot better about all that.

Joseph Redfearn

Preface

In writing about psychotherapy and ageing, I have not set out to write a definitive book on the subject. This is a personal account of how it feels to grow old, both for therapist and patient, in and out of the transference, during and after therapy. Having finished the book (and I think it must be usual to write the preface at the end, even though placing it at the beginning) I feel I should introduce myself, especially as I am not a well-known writer, and give some reasons for what I have done.

I trained with the Guild of Psychotherapists, late enough in my life to feel sympathy and some identification with the people I decided to write about. I was in my fifties when I had an 80-year-old referred to me and the years spent with her helped me with my own ageing. After this experience, I let it be known that I would like to work with older people and some interesting referrals followed. In my present practice, none are over 80 but I usually find myself seeing a fair proportion in their sixties and seventies and, although some get frightened off and use age as a reason not to continue, this does not happen significantly more often than with a younger age group. The others currently in therapy with me are mostly middle-aged. Only one is in his twenties.

My training was pluralist. Some refer to it as eclectic. It turned out to be Freudian and Object Relations oriented – with a smattering of phenomenology – rather than Jungian. My first mentors were Eric Rayner, Ben Churchill and John Heaton, who each, in their different ways, gave me the confidence to get started; and I have internalized so much of their wisdom that I find myself repeating their actual words to students whom I now supervise. The only Jungian influences during my training were my first two interviewers, Joseph Redfearn and Camilla Bosanquet, who were among the Guild's founders. If they had not accepted me on one of the first Guild courses, a lot would never have happened to me and I certainly would not have written this book. I have since been drawn more and more to the Jungian scene, as the book clearly shows. I suspect this has something to do with getting older.

In my text, I sometimes write about 'analysis', sometimes about 'therapy'. This is not entirely random but mostly depends on whether I am describing my own or someone else's work. In describing my own, I allow myself (and it seems I am allowed) to use the adjective analytic, although I do not call myself an analyst, either in the Freudian or Jungian sense. It may be queried – what is the difference? Some would say it depends on frequency of sessions and duration of treatment, and argue that, in once-weekly sessions, issues of transference/countertransference will not be worked through. But not everyone would agree.

Psychotherapy is often used as an umbrella term to include exploration and analysis of the unconscious based on the theories of different schools. It is also seen as supportive treatment for suffering individuals. People go into analysis to find out more about themselves and, in some cases, because they want to train as analysts or therapists, their motives being curiosity and a search for meaning. Others seek therapy (and also analysis) because their lives have become unbearable and they want to rid themselves of crippling neurosis. But there is an obvious overlap. No one is totally free from neurosis. Most of us, who are trained as analytic psychotherapists, find ourselves analysing, supporting and hoping for psychic change, and this applies whether we see patients once or five times a week, for months or for years. And I would like to add, as Jung strongly emphasized, that both the two people concerned need to be involved in the process and that nothing transformative can come about unless these two are willing to get hurt, take risks and be open to surprise. I hope I may be able to show some of these risks and surprises in the following pages.

PART I

The Receding Wave

Through the great song return no more
There's keen delight in what we have:
The rattle of pebbles on the shore
Under the receding wave.

(W.B. Yeats, *The Twentieth Century and After*)

CHAPTER 1

Ageing and Ageism

Any discussion of older people and their suitability for therapy, or any other kind of help, needs to be undertaken within the context of what is happening in our culture today. Sometimes we see headlines about an 'elderly crisis'. We hear of global increases in the number of old and retired in figures that leap by thousands in the course of a few days. Most of us find these statistics hard to take in. More worrying, and likely to disturb us, are the television programmes that quite frequently zoom into view about old people being neglected or ill-treated, and we hope that such publicity will lead to closures of institutions and prosecution of abusers. Perhaps we comfort ourselves with the thought that only extreme cases are newsworthy and that these extremes are not the norm. But there is a lot of sensation on the media that is likely to shock us, not only the plight of the old but the abuse of children and also of young animals, crated for slaughter overseas. With so much helplessness continually being presented to us in pictures we cannot react to it all, only to that which stirs our emotions and evokes a response, a response which is, to a great extent, unconscious and depends on our own perception of ageing and diminishment.

For two years running, 1994 and 1995, we have been presented with pictures of D-Day and VE Day survivors, all now in their seventies and eighties, many of them returning to their theatres of war, talking, reliving and remembering. The pictures showed them as they are now, interspersed with how they looked 50 years ago, smooth young faces not easily recognizable as the grandfather figures that they have now become. To meet again after such a gap must always be a shock. But the actual process of ageing is gentle and, in the absence of sudden disease, the changes are mercifully slow and not necessarily ugly. Individuals, like our culture, grow without knowing that they do so, until, with hindsight, we all perceive a difference.

To understand, perhaps to help, and certainly to learn from, an older generation, we need to take a look at history.

Being young 50 years ago was paradoxically both exciting and frustrating; exciting because of the uncertainties of war and early hints of a changing social pattern; frustrating because of wartime restrictions, as for instance rationing and no foreign travel except towards the battlefield, as well as the strict conventions of a pre-war upbringing.

In the 1930s, when today's pensioners were children, worry about the impending cataclysm was confined to those few who were, so to speak, 'in the know': the country's leaders, their families and those of the general public who read their newspapers, listened to the BBC and paid more attention to cinema newsreels than to the escapist adventures that most people preferred. Real-life horror belonged to the past. After all, there had been a war-to-end-war and the League of Nations sat securely in Geneva, ensuring peace for evermore, or so those Thirties children were taught to believe.

Families were usually less scattered; great aunts and uncles abounded, for they dated from Victorian times before birth control was generally accepted, and, provided they survived infancy, were much in evidence, as were their progeny, one's parents' cousins. What is now called the nuclear family had already become smaller and was likely to consist of one or two siblings, with perhaps a handful of one's own generation of cousins living nearby. Dutifully one visited grandparents and was, in turns, petted and ignored. One spent a lot of time being 'seen and not heard' while one's elders conducted the only conversations of any importance. There was no escape into another room to watch television. The old, like the poor, were always with us. Often one was bored, sometimes rebuked for not speaking loudly enough to be heard by the deaf. From the point of view of expecting one's thoughts and activities to be seriously acknowledged, the generation gap was huge. But the family, as a multi-layered edifice, provided a seemingly unshakable security. Being alone and unwanted were possibilities not to be contemplated, except, that is, in rare incidences, only read about in novels or occasional newspaper reports.

But were these old people really as old as one thought? Statistics tell us that 2000 years ago, one in ten lived to be 50, that by 1900, this half century was achieved by 50 per cent of the population, and that, today, two-thirds will reach 80 and beyond. In the present generation, the over-eighties are capable of a life-style comparable to the sixties and sixty-fives of 20 years ago. So the old are still very much 'with us', but it seems to be their turn to be 'seen and not heard'. Hence the paradox. We treat our older people with none of the respect accorded to those much younger, but seemingly older, grandparents and great aunts who reigned supreme in the heyday of the twentieth century. Today's oldies lack confidence. Whereas their parents were content, after 60, to wear sombre colours, little or no make-up and allow their hair to whiten, today's insistence that only youth is important has made 'you don't look your age' the one great compliment that every older person longs to hear.

One wonders – should it be a compliment? Looking back on our own lives, would we really choose (if such choice could be magically offered) to relive our twenties, with the youthful look but none of that hard-gained worldly wisdom that we may have picked up since?

What we easily accept in babies – dribbling and incontinence – we turn away from with barely disguised disgust when our elders begin to exhibit the same lack of control. Perhaps we feel guilty. Possibly our feelings affect the old people from whom we turn away, adding to their shame and dismay. We need to look beyond a beauty that is only skin-deep and to listen, while there is still time, to the mass of history that is stored in those old minds. People in their nineties (of whom there are more and more) have lived through the reigns of five English monarchs, as well as two world wars and the rise and fall of both Nazi and communist regimes, watched cars replacing horses and the whole history of air travel. Most have adapted amazingly to revolutionary change. And yet, we have somehow absorbed a pervasive myth that the old are rigid and unadaptable.

Adult Development, a book by two American psychoanalysts, Nemiroff and Colarusso, devotes a chapter to 'Myths about the Ageing Body' (Nemiroff and Colarusso 1981, pp.17–18). From studies of the adult body and brain over a length of time, they found no signs that intelligence starts a slow decline from the mid-twenties to the end of life. On the contrary, they came to the surprising conclusion that, given a normal degree of physical health and mental activity, intelligence actually increases in most individuals, as they move through their sixties, seventies and eighties. Evidence of the truth of this is reflected in such institutions as the Open University and The University of the Third Age. The brain is now seen as capable of structural modification resulting from psycho-logical stimulation and its continuing use. We need to be most particularly aware, in older people, of the complex relationship between body and mind, for, inevitably, the body will go through as many changes after the menopause (and its male equivalent) as at the onset of puberty. In fact, adolescent change and menopausal change have much in common. It is also of great importance to remember that, although, at any age, we live in our bodies, and need intact brains to exist effectively in the only world we know, there is also, for each individual, a special story, with patterns that both repeat and renew themselves as life gets longer, and that its meaning, is for most of us, not confined to the growth and deterioration of physical cells.

In a later chapter, we will look at what it actually feels like to be old, but, as a person's self-image depends on how he is seen by others, it should be salutary to take a glimpse at society's attitude and why this has become so negative. 'Ageism' is a relatively new word which we have sadly to compare with racism and sexism in its definition of prejudice and stereotype. It was coined in America by the gerontologist, Robert N. Butler, who has this to say:

> Ageism allows those of us who are younger to see old people as
> 'different'. We subtly cease to identify with them as human beings, which
> enables us to feel more comfortable about our neglect and dislike of
> them… Ageism is a thinly disguised attempt to avoid the personal reality
> of human ageing and death. (Butler 1975, p.893–900)

Old people are a threat. It is easier to turn them into a different species and
exile them to a far country so that they do not contaminate the young with
their (imagined) terminal disease, the disease of old age. And is there not also,
on the part of the young, some element of revenge against those who kept them
down and considered them unimportant, a sharp reminder of change in status?
It is now the young, not the old, who rule the world.

What has become of the archetypal Wise Old Man and Wise Old Woman?
Some of us still remember this dying race. We had grandparents who told us
stories. Indeed these old people actually came into the stories. There was
Cinderella's fairy godmother, Merlin, Mrs Doasyouwouldbedoneby, a whole
crowd of enlightened elders, whose job it was to understand the young and
give to them their own understanding of how life could best be lived. Is it that
today's children read different stories, are more influenced by comic pantomime
dames than by wise fairies and are accustomed to seeing old people made a
laughing-stock on the television screen? Most of us assumed, when young, that
we would learn from experience and eventually grow wise ourselves. This we
saw as an important part of human development, just as much as the growth,
reproduction and eventual demise of our bodies. Psychologically, there was
something to gain which might even outweigh the losses. We, in turn, would
become magicians and fairy godmothers.

The Jungian view of human development is through the archetypes. First
we have the fierce struggle to break away from the grip of The Mother and all
she stands for. We seek adventures through identification with The Hero, get
caught in Anima and Animus projections, dream of The Child and experience
renewal, get startled and turned upside down by The Trickster before at last
(or so we hoped) donning the mantle of the Wise Old Man or Woman.

Not so, says Doctor Guggenbuhl-Craig, determined to disillusion us:

> Wisdom of old age is dubious, but the negative sides of old age are only
> too obvious…old age loses contact with…the collective psyche…
> Between birth and the ages of thirty and forty, one is in touch with the
> reigning mythologies, images. However, as new images, mythologies
> appear, one slowly loses touch with them, one is guided by the images
> which were important when one was young – or middle-aged.
> (Guggenbuhl-Craig 1991, p.51)

He gives examples of being overtaken by fashions and new technologies. He seems to me to be talking about knowledge rather than wisdom, which takes no account of what is transient and is unaffected by trendiness. He sees old age essentially as a time of loss, diminution, dementia, and he thinks that we use the Wise Old Man/Woman archetype as a tranquillizer. Wisdom, he says, is found more often in the young and he cites Jesus as an example. There is nothing here to dispute. Some individuals become wise early, perhaps because, like Jesus, they already see their lives shaped by death. Habitually one says of a wise child, 'He is old beyond his years,' but then we speak of maturity rather than age, and it is obviously in maturity that wisdom is acquired. But some develop more slowly than others and need a long life to grow wise. Others never outgrow their foolishness.

Guggenbuhl-Craig would like us to replace the Wise Old Man/Woman with the archetype of the fool. Again there is nothing to dispute: 'Accepting this foolishness in old age, might it not be a special kind of wisdom?' (ibid.) Certainly, if one did not suspect that he finds this foolishness in age so hard to bear. He suggests that the wisdom of the old is projected on to them by the young, who, for some reason, fear to claim that wisdom for themselves. Do they? It seems to me that, in our society, quite the opposite is true. It is foolishness that gets projected, and the old, by colluding with this image, dismiss their own wisdom.

Nevertheless, the 'Wise Fool' has a distinguished pedigree. When we meet him in fairy stories, he is not always old but often the youngest son, the one who appears to be a simpleton. The mediaeval jester spoke words of wisdom disguised as nonsense and, in this way, could mock the follies of the established order. I am reminded of the popular television programme, *Waiting for God*, in which two irrepressible old people mock the ill-run retirement home in which they live, enliven it with their tricks and never mind making fools of themselves. But there is also the 'Holy Fool', who allows himself to be scorned. Parsifal is one example and so, of course, is Jesus.

Often the really old have to be exposed to degrading rituals, such as having to wear nappies and being fed like babies; so they must submit to being fools, with all the accoutrements of wisdom stripped away. Yet, with humour and humility, they manage, some of them, to hang on to a wider perspective, remembering perhaps, that the 'the foolishness of God is wiser than men' (Corinthians I, 25).

Humour is of course essential for dissipating anxiety, but only when the 'victim' refuses this role. The old can often laugh at each other and their shared jokes may relieve the boredom of comparing disabilities. The jokes may even amuse the carers, who are often tired and find the job unrewarding. They too need a bit of that lightness which shows appreciation, but it is the old and not they who should initiate the laughter. Otherwise the carers may seem to mock.

In this opening chapter and throughout the first part of the book, I am trying to depict the background that has shaped the imagination and behaviour of those who have lived through years of change, both in themselves and in the external world, and to take seriously all that has been survived as well as that which has been lost, together with new insights deserving of our attention and respect. How else can we hope to help those older than ourselves?

I am concerned with the whole range of old age, which, if we take it as belonging to the time after retirement, covers the early sixties up to the late nineties and beyond. It therefore becomes necessary to think of at least two stages which are now being called 'young old' and 'old old'. Whether the 'old old' are suitable as patients in therapy is a question that needs to be aired and cannot be decided by a blanket assessment of the years lived. But that belongs to a later chapter.

Ageing is a process that continues throughout life and I may find myself writing as much about childhood – whether chronologically or as a state of regression – as about age. Nobody is consistently mature or immature, and we keep seeing the child still very much alive in the adult, just as we also catch glimpses, quite early on, of the adult in the child.

It is worth remembering some achievements. Copernicus was 70 when he published his first and last book and founded modern astronomy. At 70, Golda Meir became prime minister of Israel. And, at 77, Gandhi won independence for India. Among my own friends, I know someone who got her degree at 67, her MA at 70 and is now working for a PhD. This late-life success is, these days, not particularly unusual.

CHAPTER 2

Does it Have to be Like This?

Growing old is as difficult as growing up, not only for the protagonist but for relatives and those who care. Material comfort, financial security, a close-knit family, all these can help to oil the wheels but, however smooth the circumstances, there can be no external guarantee that all will be well in a person's inner world. What follows is an imagined glimpse into the minds of a mother and daughter, caught in the web both of mutual good intentions and resentments. The daughter was mourning her husband's premature death. Her mother was in her nineties. My attempted 'free associations' reflect, as clearly as it is possible to know – and are also a condensation of – what each was thinking over a period of five years. The climax might well be described by the cliché phrase 'a happy release' – for both of them.

What seems disturbing about this story is that, given space, money, choice, as well as the already-mentioned good intentions, the ageing process was nevertheless so lacking in the serenity we would all hope for as we end our lives. Without so many material advantages, each might have suffered more and of course we are aware that worse prisons exist and that many daughters sacrifice themselves to a horrifying degree in living up to both their own and others' expectations of their duty.

Imagine a house divided into two, the most spacious part of it occupied only by the daughter, who kept the rooms exactly as they were when it had been a family house with husband and son and frequent visitors. She had always worked intermittently and now saw to it that her work-load increased and that she got paid help for her mother, who lived in a comfortable 'granny flat'. The door dividing them had a lock and key and, originally, a bell, which the mother never thought of using. The key seemed to have gone missing.

Here then, is my attempt to eavesdrop on their thoughts:

MOTHER: I know now why I'm having to live so long. It's to look after my daughter. She's always been my baby. I'm here to help her in her bereavement. It's nice to have a purpose. We'll go on living in this house, just the two of us. I hope she won't stop me doing things for her. She gets tired after her day's work. I'd like to take over the cooking and then we can have meals together. We can make a nice home and console each other. After all, I'm feeling the loss too. He was like a son to me, always attentive, anticipating my needs, never putting himself first.

DAUGHTER: I want Mother to stay here till she dies, even though the house is too big for us. But I find I welcome its size. There's room to get away and live my separate life. She has her own flat, just as she always did. The rest of the house is mine. I've got to keep it that way. I can't be swallowed up. Of course I'm lonely, but I've still got my way of life, our married life. I still keep saying 'we' instead of 'I'. Someone asked me the other day – did I mean myself and my mother as a pair. No, that's *not* what I meant. One day I'll go back to being just 'I' again but there's still so much mourning to go through. I can't change my identity all at once and I can't go back to being my mother's child again, as though I'd never married. I must live my life and she must live hers. I'll help her all I can, if she'll let me. But she seems to do better with paid help while I get on with my career.

MOTHER: I've got the Christmas pudding I cooked last year. We'll have to try and celebrate, even if we don't have a tree. I told them both that I'd made two puddings last Christmas just in case I died during the year. I always like to plan ahead. *He* looked me straight in the face and said, 'You haven't made the marmalade yet.' So we both laughed and of course I made the marmalade as soon as the Seville oranges came in. I made enough to last us quite a long time. *She* keeps going on diets and not eating breakfast, but I like what I make so much better than the kind you buy from the shops. I do wish she'd come and have her meals with me.

DAUGHTER: Mother found me crying alone in my room. She was very sensible. She just said quietly, 'Come and spend the evening with me.' I didn't want to but I did. I thought at first I was doing it for her sake but it helped. We talked about nothing much. I stopped crying. I wanted to say thank you but I couldn't. I think she wants me to kiss her. I used to kiss her.

They all thought I was too clinging as a child – babyish. And now she wants me to be her baby, now when it's too late. I can't call her 'darling' – I just can't. It's silly to stick on that one word. I don't know what's stopping me.

MOTHER: People say she's being brave. But sometimes she lets herself go. I could never cry in front of people. In my generation, we were brought up not to show our feelings. I'm beginning to think it's time she took a pull on herself. But it's no good my saying it. I wish she'd kiss me goodnight. She always used to. If she wants to cry, why can't she do it alone with me instead of spilling out her troubles to strangers? I'm lonely too. I don't think she realizes that. I keep thinking – it should have been me.

DAUGHTER: I wish Mother wouldn't say that. I've been trying so hard not to think it. It would be terrible to want somebody to die, especially one's mother. But of course it should have been her.

MOTHER: They're all trying to stop me doing the things I've always done – offering to go to the shops, water the garden, help in the kitchen. Why can't they leave me to get on with it? I just want to carry on as usual, in my own way.

DAUGHTER: Old people have a way of standing in the doorway when you're in a hurry. You can't get round them and they don't hear when you try and tell them you're there. Then you have to shout and it sounds rude.

MOTHER: She doesn't have to shout, only to look at me when she talks. I wish she wasn't so impatient, always in a hurry. She's in and out of the room before I've taken in what she came to say.

DAUGHTER: And now she's had a fall and broken her arm. I tried so hard to look after her but she criticized everything I did. She was furious with herself and took it out on me. In the end we had to get a nurse.

MOTHER: I hate all this fuss. I can manage – with a little help. But I do dislike other people's cooking.

DAUGHTER: I went to a lot of trouble to give her a really nice meal but she'd made up her mind beforehand that she wasn't going to like it. She's frustrated because she wanted it the other

way round, her looking after me. She's got an enormous
need to be needed. What she doesn't realize is – so have I!
I'm beginning to think perhaps she's envious. It's hard to
think of my lot as enviable. But I'm younger and stronger
and my work's interesting. Her days must be pretty boring.
And then – sometimes I forget – she's a widow too. How
ordinary it is to be a widow – how boringly ordinary and
how bloody awful!

MOTHER: They think I'm just a silly old woman – no use to anyone
any more. I'm holding her back. I thought I could help but
I'm just holding her back. She wants me to sit still like a
vegetable in case I fall down again. But I'd rather risk it.
What sort of life is this?

DAUGHTER: I thought old age was supposed to be serene. Sometimes I
just hate watching her, thinking I'll be like that one day. My
God – I'd rather die first.

MOTHER: She doesn't know how empty life is. My eyes aren't up to
much reading or sewing. It can't be good for me just to sit
in my chair and doze. I've always been active – always.

DAUGHTER: I thought they liked watching television.

MOTHER: It goes too fast. I can't follow these modern plays.

DAUGHTER: I wish they did more classic serials. She only understands
when she knows the story already.

MOTHER: I've got my memories. I can't travel any more but I've got
picture books. And there's my garden – I'm still in charge of
that. The seasons come and go very quickly. Each year I
wonder if I'll get through another winter. I wonder if it's
worth the effort. But then the blossom's out again and I'm
glad I've lived to see it.

DAUGHTER: Just as well I'm not interested in gardening. It looks lovely
but Dick does it all and she's the one who pays. She loves
pottering round with him. It's the highlight of her week.
We had a strip of garden once. Not much grew but
sometimes I think I appreciated it more. Here, she won't let
me pick the flowers.

MOTHER: I wish she had more time to sit and talk. I'm proud of her. I
tell everyone I'm proud of the work she's doing.

DAUGHTER: She never respected me. She doesn't understand my work and it's no good trying to explain. She'd much rather talk about the family, especially when anything goes wrong. And she doesn't like it if I disagree.

MOTHER: I wish she wouldn't argue. Sometimes she quite frightens me – always having to be right.

DAUGHTER: I wish we could have a discussion. It's pointless just cooing at each other, as if I have to agree that everything she says is unquestionably right. I think I'm already mourning the person she used to be.

MOTHER: She bought me a machine – wanted me to talk to it. She said she'd like a record of the past. I felt she was treating me as dead already. Can't she see I want to live in the present? There's not much time left.

DAUGHTER: She always expects me to drop everything I'm doing and attend to whatever she wants at this moment. Perhaps she thinks there won't be time tomorrow. Yes, that's it – no tomorrow. I ought to understand. It's awful this irritation that comes over me, and how being irritated hampers compassion. I feel guilty all the time.

MOTHER: We used to be such a happy family. But now she seems to think I didn't understand her.

DAUGHTER: Of course she was a good mother. But I can't go on being her baby daughter all my life. I ought to be looking after her and I feel guilty because I don't.

MOTHER: I feel so useless and everyone treats me like a child.

DAUGHTER: Which of us is the child?

MOTHER: The young don't know about being old.

DAUGHTER: She's got her religion.

MOTHER: She won't take me to church, thinks I'll catch cold. *She's* the one who feels the cold.

DAUGHTER: The vicar comes, but she says it's not the same. I think she's proud of being the oldest in that congregation. She likes to show off.

MOTHER: I've lived too long, outlived my usefulness. But it's hard to think about dying. I can't plan for the next world because I

don't know what it will be like, and I'm so used to making
plans. I keep forgetting things – it's rather frightening.
People come and tidy my papers and I don't know where
anything is. And my clothes – she borrowed my best coat –
she thinks I gave it to her. As if I'd give her my best coat.

DAUGHTER: She gave me her coat and then she forgot. Now I don't want
to give it back. She never wears it and it's hardly worth my
buying a new one. But that's an awful thing to say. Oh, why
must I feel so guilty all the time?

MOTHER: There's such a lot I can't remember. I'd rather die before
everything goes blank. When I caught flu or whatever it
was, I thought – why do I have to get better only to die all
over again? But here I am, struggling through my nineties
and being treated like a naughty child.

DAUGHTER: Old age is such a struggle. Must it always be like this? I wish
she'd stop fighting it – just let go and let people take over.

MOTHER: Why did I have to live so long? I thought I knew, thought
there was a reason – but I seem to forget what it was. Let go
– they all say, let go, leave it to God.

DAUGHTER: Sometimes I think she'd rather die. It's her body that won't
let her. It's a sort of instinct, I suppose, to resist giving in.
But does it always have to be like this? Will I be the same, I
wonder.

None of this was said aloud. There were two monologues but no dialogue; or,
one might say there was superficial chatter, what the daughter's husband used
to call 'twittering' between two personas or (in Winnicott's terminology) 'false
selves'.

To be fair, there was the occasional breakthrough. There was a memorable
occasion when the daughter attended a weekend workshop (intended to help
the bereaved) during which she refused to let off steam by tearing up old
telephone directories or banging on the floor, crying and screaming at some
image of her hated mother. Instead she turned her hatred on the group
facilitator. After driving back, in a dazed condition and much too fast, she did,
for an evening, become quite childishly affectionate to her mother, who, in
some bewilderment, held her hand. 'I don't hate you, Mother, I don't hate you.'
'Of course you don't, darling, whatever gave you that idea?'

In her late nineties, after struggling to weed the garden and cope with her
correspondence, which she often gazed at blankly, leaving bills unpaid or

cheques unsigned, the mother eventually collapsed and had to be put to bed. She became disorientated.

MOTHER: Where am I? Where have they taken me?

DAUGHTER: *(aloud)* You're in your bedroom, Mother. No one's sending you away. You're in your own house with all your things. And, just now, I'm here with you, Mother – darling!

At last she had managed to say the word on which she had stuck so long. Fighting the dominant old woman, 'darling' had not seemed the appropriate epithet. Now, diminished and dependent, with little sight left, her mother had turned into a pathetic child who invited compassion.

When she actually died, it was one of those rare occasions, where the death was met with a welcome. She sat up suddenly and smiled. Then she just said, 'Ah!' and fell back on her pillows, still smiling. Her death was seen only by an attendant nurse. The daughter was at work. But she had already said goodbye when her mother was conscious and could hear what she said. She even managed a stuttered 'thank you' for good (or at least 'good enough') mothering.

A common assumption might be that not only the mother, but the daughter too, were well past the age of being suitable subjects for psychotherapy, but, reading between the lines, not of their actual dialogue, but what we have guessed to be their conscious thoughts, it is not difficult to glimpse some of the unresolved conflicts in both lives which kept them from sharing feelings openly with each other. How to bridge the generation gap is a perennial difficulty but, with a little therapeutic help – ideally for each of them separately – more honesty might have been achieved in acknowledging mixtures of love and hate, as only to be expected, rather than guilt at not experiencing a mutually constant love.

It would be interesting to construct a case history for each of these 'patients', by looking at differences and similarities in their backgrounds, thereby attempting to throw some light on this mother and daughter struggle that became so painfully reactivated late in life.

The mother had been the eldest of a big family in which her own mother was subject to unpredictable mood swings. These sometimes got out of control, with phases of manic activity when she would impose on her children all sorts of projects, in which they did not always want to participate. It was up to the eldest daughter to keep the family running smoothly and look after her younger siblings. This responsibility was never acknowledged by her Victorian father, who depended on her to augment the mothering and also to deny that there was any need to do so. Outwardly she had to honour her father and mother. The older generation must be seen to be in charge. She loved and respected her father and loyally played the role he gave her. Clashes with her mother brought on guilt and anger which had to be repressed.

A change of scene at 15 resulted in a decision to send her to boarding-school. Over this she was not consulted. The school was rigid and authoritarian. She quickly became tearful and showed such distress that her father decided to take her away. This must have been one of the few times in her life when she felt frighteningly out of control. She was also ashamed at her failure, especially as her younger sister thrived within the school's strict boundaries. With the support of a more easygoing school, she succeeded in 'pulling herself together' and from then on gained a lifelong reputation for strength. She was proud of being the sort of person on whom others could rely. In practical ways, she was the stronger partner in her marriage. Her husband enjoyed being helpless in the home though he was outstandingly effective outside it. She had postnatal depression when her first child was born and this must have awakened some of the earlier panic. However, she recovered as soon as the child was weaned and was relieved at being able to attribute her depression to physical causes. She subsequently weaned her second daughter after three weeks, assuming that what suited her also suited the baby and there is no evidence that this is not so. Both babies were thoroughly looked after and, during their childhood, she would probably have been seen as a model mother. She was respected by all her relations for her good sense and practicality and she had a big part to play behind the scenes in her husband's successful career. She seldom, if ever, complained of any weakness. During the menopause, she had severe headaches; this coincided with her younger daughter's puberty, during which time the daughter also had headaches. The mother never allowed herself – as she would have put it – to 'give way' to illness but was kinder to her daughter whom she enjoyed looking after.

She and her husband celebrated their golden wedding a year before he died. It was a big family gathering.

Most of her long widowhood was spent in her younger daughter's house. The elder daughter lived and worked overseas. 'Family' had dwindled in size. She had had five brothers and sisters, all of whom died before she did. Her younger daughter produced, rather late, one grandson. Thus, for some years, the mother lived in a three-generation house, as its senior inhabitant, doing her own housekeeping and in sole charge of the shared garden, continuing, as already described, into her late nineties. She became shaky on her legs, with deafness and memory loss, but no sign of senility. She was generally admired. Her relations had always referred to her as 'wonderful'. She could be autocratic with 'servants' or nurses, but was appreciated by those who, in her extreme old age, allowed her to take risks in preserving her precious independence.

Looking at the daughter's childhood, there are obvious differences. She was the youngest, so there were no more babies to look after. She was on the receiving end, always junior. Spoilt? Certainly her mother would have tried to live up to some ideal of mothering that she, herself, had missed. She would have aimed at consistency and there was in all probability, consistency of mood, but she was not able to provide a stable home in the sense of staying in one place. Her husband's career took him abroad and the daughter started travelling before she was a year old. At six, she was sent to boarding-school; too young, it would have been assumed, to be consulted. She survived this and other upheavals without the obvious breakdown that the mother had suffered at her school, though by the time the daughter reached her teens, she felt herself to be living in two worlds with different behaviours required for each. Talking to her parents was like using a foreign language and she almost gave up trying. Her silence was observed with amusement rather than concern. It was described as a 'phase' that she would 'get through'. This proved right and she gradually recovered her power of speech but was left with the feeling that the failure in communication was entirely her own fault as was her inability to fulfil her parents' expectations. It was not that they expected much, probably too little, but what they wanted was never clear. Her mother continued to give her things. Even opinions were handed to her ready-made. Her rather uncertain disagree-ments she kept secret, slowly, painfully, setting up boundaries in which to become a separate person. All through her childhood, she protected her fragile ego with secrets, keeping her thoughts and opinions safe from adult contami-nation. One is reminded perhaps of Jung, when, as a child, he carved a little image of himself which he hid under the floorboards to take out and hold when he felt the need.

When the daughter married, she found herself respected and this was a new experience. Her husband also respected her parents. They had never had a son and he had lacked loving parents. The two couples were happy together. The daughter and husband lived according to the pattern they made for themselves, which was very different from that of the daughter's parents. Domestic jobs were shared and the house was, on the whole, more important than work. The husband had a fluctuating career and retired early.

At the age of eight, their only son went to boarding-school, thus repeating a family pattern, but also the pattern of his choice. Being an only child, he was keen to mix with his peers. Later he got caught in the public school system and was not given much chance to opt out. He never said he wanted to. There must have been, as for his mother, a difficult transition to make at the end of every term. When he got tongue-tied, his mother finished his sentences for him, just as her mother had finished hers. Then she caught herself doing it and tried not to. It seems that, despite our endeavours to change, we tend to treat our children the way our parents treated us.

The daughter's husband never reached old age. They celebrated their silver wedding a year before he died. It was a happy family occasion with three generations present. The guests were mostly cousins.

The son, in his late thirties, shows no sign of wanting to get married and the family continues to dwindle. His mother is prepared to be open with him but, when it comes to expressing feelings, his mouth is tightly shut.

How do we cross the generation gap?

Since I am writing about ageing, I shall concentrate on the mother/daughter dynamics without pursuing what may have been handed on to the son, who would not, at his age, be considered unsuitable for therapy, were he to ask for it. Fortunately this daughter managed several years of therapy for herself, which is why I am able to explore some of the power struggle that went on between her and her mother. She always regretted not having had the experience earlier, which would have meant an appropriate adolescent rebellion at a time when her mother was strong enough to cope with the backlash, rather than having to face her daughter's long-delayed resentment so near the end of her life.

The important issues seem to be about family solidarity, what constitutes weakness and strength and what can never be spoken.

Comparing the mother and daughter's respective infancies, it seems clear that the daughter had a better start. The mother actually enjoyed mothering and worked at making her babies happy. It was the father who absented himself, in contrast to the mother's father, who was omnipresent. The daughter was not given responsibilities before she was ready for them, nor did she have to enter into games of pretence to protect adult neurosis. Although subjected to greater upheavals at an early age and being sent away at six, she never suffered the humiliating breakdown that so frightened her mother at 15. Without that fear, she could be flexible, not rigid or controlling in her dealings with people. Often she allowed herself to be weak and indulge in the luxury of being looked after, even rather spoilt. The drawback was that she complied too much with family standards of behaviour and denied opinions of her own. Too much looking after made her helpless and unaware that she had any freedom of choice. Almost it seemed easier to choose not to choose. Mothering, though undoubtedly 'good enough', was on her mother's terms, as though the decision to wean her at three weeks, to suit her mother and therefore, it was presumed, herself, was repeated time and again. The mother knew best. The family knew best. All those caring relatives could not be argued with.

Marriage was a release. She found herself respected at last as an independent being with ideas worth listening to. She became less a second-hand person, though she still lacked confidence and was over sensitive when she failed or seemed not to be heard. Her husband once said to her, 'You may bend but you'll never break.' He made her see that the mother, for all her strength, had, on two occasions, broken. When her husband died, her grief was intense and she realized how dependent she had continued to be, hence her desperate need not to be 'swallowed up' by the mother. But she did not reach breaking-point.

As the mother grew older and weaker, the daughter was ashamed at feeling triumph, ruthlessness and, above all, guilt.

Impossible to think that in *her* family, mothers and daughters could fail to love each other. It took her a long time to differentiate what she had been taught to feel and what she actually experienced herself feeling.

Do we need to lose our parents in order to grow up? The answer must, I think, be 'yes', but not necessarily by death.

If, in life, we can learn when to be close and when to keep our distance, and if, across the generations, we can manage a little more honesty and respect for each other's separateness, perhaps there is hope, even in families, of being as ageless as we often are, quite naturally, with strangers.

CHAPTER 3

Reinventing Self

'I find great pressure to be inventive and reinventive of different versions of self,' says Robert Butler, '...a continuing lifelong crisis is a sign of good health... Human beings need the freedom to change, to invent and reinvent themselves a number of times throughout life' (Butler 1978, p.219).

How, we find ourselves asking, can we possibly invent ourselves. Who we are depends on so many things outside our control, genes, the place and time of birth, as well as the emotional and material state of our parents, who did not necessarily will this chancy event. We never asked to be born. Existence was forced on us.

And yet, unless psychotic, or perhaps demented, we have a sense of something we call 'self'. What exactly we mean when we say 'myself' as distinct from 'yourself' is baffling in the extreme and, reading the literature, we find that we are confronted with a maze of models, none of which can do more than act as aids in defining self-experience. The psychoanalyst Kohut, in his *The Restoration of the Self* (Kohut 1977), admits that he can give no definition and that we can only know the self through its manifestations. In this, he comes surprisingly near to the thought of Jung, who included, in these manifestations, archetypal experience. The Jungian self comprises the totality of the psyche, unconscious as well as conscious and, as such, our experience of it at any one time can only be partial. And yet, however limited, we hang on to self-experience – our sense of identity – throughout our lives and may even see it as our only certainty in a shifting world.

If, as Bettelheim passionately argues, Freud's 'id', 'ego' and 'superego' had been translated as the 'it', the 'I' and the 'upper I' and our 'mental apparatus' allowed to be called 'soul', as he claims Freud intended, how, I wonder, would self-experience have been affected? 'No word has greater and more immediate connotations than the pronoun "I". It is one of the most frequently used words in spoken language – and, more important, it is the most personal word' (Bettelheim 1983, p.53).

Nevertheless, any English-speaking child, recognizing itself for the first time in the mirror, will proclaim, 'that's me'. In this simple statement, there seems to be a dualism. 'I', the subject, looks at 'me', the object, and, perhaps with some surprise, the observer feels not quite at one with the observed. Is this just a colloquial use of the language, which, through persistent habit, has ceased to be ungrammatical, or does its very use imply a recognition that one's sense of identity operates on two levels? The acquisition of consciousness involves, at an early stage, consciousness of self as an object in the outside world, recognized by others and called by a name, as well as self, the emerging 'I', that wants, and desperately needs, to be given this recognition.

The dualism encountered by the infant, as well as every individual of whatever age who looks in the mirror, is the result of two differing experiences, the one fragmentary and the other whole. The reflected 'whole' image, which I described as 'me', shows a body, with a distinct shape, occupying its own space in a world of other 'me's'. 'I' greets 'me' as an intact body that moves easily in this shared world. But the infant 'I' has not yet mastered its body; it inhabits uncoordinated limbs and organs rather than the unity which the mirrored 'me' shows. Like Narcissus, 'I' falls in love with 'me'.

According to Lacan, 'The mirror stage is a drama whose internal thrust is precipitated from insufficiency to anticipation' (Lacan 1966, p.68). It seems that any notion of permanence is illusory and the human 'subject' (which Lacan calls neither the 'ego' nor the 'self') is bound to be disappointed.

This dualism of an inner 'I' and an outer 'me' persists, for most of us, through youth into age, surviving and developing in the face of enormous bodily and mental change.

The infant loves the mirror image as an ideal. The ageing adult, unaware of a changing body (unless ill or in pain), loves the memory of that image and is able, most of the time, to use the mirror for practical purposes, looking at, but not seeing, alteration in a body that has for so long been taken for granted. What comes as a shock is any unexpected meeting, such as in a shop window, or in photographs, with an unrecognizably old body. The dualism is acute. So the infantile recognition is reversed.

The new image is far from ideal, and the old person's narcissism, which still persists, is now internal and in contradiction with the outer 'me'. We become alienated from our bodies, strangers to ourselves. Butler, the gerontologist already quoted, gives an extreme illustration:

> Another patient, eighty-six years old and periodically confused, often stood before the mirror in his hospital room and rhythmically chanted either happily or angrily. He was especially given to angry flare-ups and crying spells over food, money and clothes. When angry he would screech obscenities at his mirror image, so savagely beating his fist upon

a nearby table that the staff tried to protect him by covering the mirror…
(He) denied that the image was himself, and when an observer came up
beside him and said, 'See, this is me in the mirror and there you are in
the mirror', he smiled and said, 'That's you in the mirror all right, but
that's not me.' (Butler 1963, p.68)

There is, of course, another mirror, that of society, which, in our culture, holds
very negative images of age.

But an old person's rejection of the body has its positive side. Our bodies
are not the whole of ourselves but might be seen as temporary habitations
which, in time, wear out and die. With the death of the body, and, in my opinion,
almost certainly, the death of individual consciousness, where, we may ask, and
what *are* these mysterious selves? Or is the concept of 'self' an illusion?

The very young and the very old, who, removed from the business and
busyness of the middle years, are perhaps more apt to ponder on life's mysteries,
may ask themselves the same sort of questions – 'Who am I?' 'Why am I in the
world?' But, whereas the child may speculate about where he came from, the
old person will probably worry about the final destination. These questions are
not answerable in factual terms, only experientially in what we recognize and
in what we can share; as well as in using language, which is symbolic. We make
sense of things and we communicate that sense to others through the telling
of stories. Listening to other people's stories puts us in touch with numerous
alternative inventions. Some stories are familiar; others remain strange, but, even
in their strangeness, open us to a range of choices and possibilities. Telling
stories gives us a sense of continuity. And, if we look into the world's mythology,
we will see how the same themes have expressed human concerns since
prehistory. This is not surprising when we consider how little the important
crises in our development differ from one person to another. In the same way
as there is said to be only a limited supply of plots available for the writing of
novels, we each of us in our lives replay all sorts of variations of the same story,
right through from birth, separation, leaving home, puberty, work, sex, pro-
creation, ageing and certain death; a rich and yet limited range of archetypal
images accompanies this process.

Although old people are renowned for their vivid memories of childhood,
compared with much vaguer memories of yesterday, even the early memories
can become unreal. Because a patchwork of pictures has always been available,
one reaches a stage of simply remembering that one remembers. What these
pictures represent has grown dim and it is like looking at faded photographs.
The picture is familiar but sometimes one has forgotten the feelings that went
with it. Like the young child, we again experience fragmentation. There is
discrepancy between the body glimpsed in the mirror, the actual contents of
the family album, which is black and white, yellowing, possibly blurred and

out of focus; between the liveliness of our wishes and the draining of physical energy. There is also the seeming acceleration of days, weeks, years, of time running unbelievably away. We thought, perhaps, that we had trapped a little of the past, and of ourselves, in the old albums, but only a few, still living relatives, perhaps siblings or cousins, are able to identify those sturdy infants or slender teenagers as our greying selves; and it is a shock when more recent friends exclaim, 'Did you really look like that?' Or, 'I assumed your hair was fair.' It is difficult, in the face of other people's disbelief, to hang on to that experiential continuity, which is concomitant with freedom of choice and reinvention.

In struggling to maintain a coherent existence, we may find ourselves haunted by quite threatening images of fragmentation. A patient in her sixties had a disturbing dream in which a professor assembled pieces of junk to make a pattern on the floor. As she watched, the pieces turned into displaced body organs which he kept rearranging to make a bizarre image of a woman, which he called 'The Mother'. A child ran about in agitation, laughing, playing and also screaming. In the medley of changing shapes, the child turned from a boy into a girl, and the dreamer, instead of being an observer, became partly identified with the child, but also with the mother whose body was in pieces on the floor. There was an intense curiosity, tinged with fear, about what was going on in the mother's body, seemingly broken and perhaps killed by this all-powerful professor. She woke in panic, hardly daring to move for fear of finding herself in pieces, but gradually a feeling of wholeness came back to her, as she regained conscious control of her limbs and the choice to forget the dream or remember and write it down so that she could think about it at a time of her choosing. If her therapist had given only an Oedipal interpretation without allowing for mystery, she would have felt robbed of that freedom. As it was, they were able to wonder about it together.

Fate needs to be distinguished from destiny, that which is pre-determined from that which we may be able to challenge or transform. To grasp our destiny, we need solid foundations. Winnicott has given us the image of 'transitional object', initially the special rag or toy that occupies the space between infant and mother and which, later, through play, extends to culture and creativity. A 74 four-year-old patient chews his handkerchief every morning as a comforter to help him face the day. He had a lot of early separations from his mother. Is it too late, I wonder, to hope that his object may become less transitional as he manages a less persecutory and more creative stance? Christopher Bollas has added to Winnicott's concept the term 'transformational object':

> That the infant identified the mother with transformation of being, through his symbiotic knowing, is not a delusion, but a fact; the mother actually transforms the infant's world... The acquisition of language is

> perhaps the most obvious…but learning to handle an object, to differentiate…to remember objects that are not present, are transformative achievements: they result in ego change that alters the nature of the infant's object world. (Bollas 1986, p.85)

Through the mother's transformational capacity, the infant is able to make use of the environment and fulfil his destiny. It is only, says Rayner (following Winnicott), if

> the individual's true self has been lost and he is at the mercy of his compliance with environmental demands, then, Bollas suggests, he is fated. A person who finds his destiny is actively discovering aspects of the environment to use creatively in fulfilment of his potentials that is his destiny. In contrast, when a person is fated he is passively driven by forces that are outside his foresight and span of decision. (Rayner 1991, pp.82–83)

Fulfilling our destiny, rather than submitting to fate, suggests the possibility of choice, creativity, invention and reinvention of what we are and what we can become. This becoming is, to the Jungian, the task of individuation and Jung saw this as belonging to the second half of life. A generation later, Fordham has come up with the concept of a primary self, as a totality, not only to be discovered in adult life, but potentially ours in infancy, before there can be any meaningful experience of individual identity. From virtual unconsciousness, separation comes through a process of what he calls 'deintegration' (not to be confused with disintegration), followed by a necessary 'reintegration', a to and fro movement which is repeated throughout life. Rosemary Gordon has given us an analogy of this process: 'When I try to describe, to myself and others, the relationship of Fordham's primary self to Jung's big self, the image that comes to mind is of a single fertilized cell, which, after innumerable divisions, opens out into a living organism endowed with many diverse functions' (Gordon 1993, p.146). The deintegrating process separates bit by bit what is individual from its genetic inheritance and builds up the infant ego. But developing a strong ego is not our ultimate aim. Growing old brings with it a gradual surrender of what we have taken such pains to produce, that very small conscious part of the whole, which we have come to identify with the phrase 'I am'. And I am referring here, not to that numinous I AM, spoken to Moses (though some may experience a hint of this through mystical experience), but, more modestly, to all those partial 'I am's' which come and go in the course of our exclusive but myopic dramas; and of the danger of inflating the ego, by which we mean blowing up what is partial and mistaking it for the whole.

Often, looking back, we see various stages of our lives as self-contained and having nothing much to do with each other. School, for instance, is a microcosm of the larger world, with its own beginning, middle and end. Marriage also occupies a period of time and, whether long or short, it is likely to cover our most productive years. When it finishes, we mourn, either the death of a person, or the death of the marriage, divorce often feeling as much like amputation as widowhood. Long afterwards, provided we have managed to move on, the lost partnership will become remote. However close the original involvement, both our immediate environment and the world itself will have changed, leaving important events unshared. We may find ourselves looking back on the old life with some surprise, almost as a previous incarnation. Could that timid, or that strongly protective, person really have been me? The same might be said if we spend several years in analysis, for, here, we experience another intimate relationship, which is born, develops and dies. This may be a time when our dreams inform our waking life and, how easily with no one to hear about them, we forget them and let them go, another loss. Analysis is an intensely lived experience and, if it influences and changes us, we cannot escape mourning its end. We remember it with nostalgia, and also some relief, as a time of growing up, of comfort in loneliness, of having someone to help us make sense of things. It is also a time for making connections between those separated microcosms, for reliving infancy and youth so that we can move on to further staging posts without losing sight of what we have had to leave behind. Getting older, we collect more and more microcosms to fit into the jigsaw of an eventful life. Sometimes it is hard to see a pattern in such a muddle of pieces.

Robert Butler, and others in the USA, have applied a technique which they call 'Life Review' for the purpose of encouraging the telling of stories and the linking of all those separated reminiscences just mentioned. Butler describes 'a naturally occurring universal mental process characterized by the progressive return to consciousness of past experiences and, particularly, the resurgence of unresolved conflicts; simultaneously, and normally, these experiences and conflicts can be surveyed and reintegrated' (Butler 1963, pp.65–76). This 'naturally occurring process' can be deliberately evoked, often with the aid of photographs and other memorabilia, which the patient brings to sessions. He or she is encouraged to produce some sort of taped or written autobiography, to go on pilgrimages, either in person or through correspondence, to rediscover places and people connected with the past. Tracing family roots is another aid, especially perhaps for Americans. 'One of the ways the old seem to resolve fears of death is to gain a sense of other family members who have died before them' (Butler and Lewis 1974, p.165). A systematic 'Life Review' can take on an amazing intensity. Nemiroff and Colarusso, in their book *The Race against Time*, report a patient as saying 'It's as though it happened only yesterday,' and '"I felt as though I was there.".' The clarity of these reminiscences extends to striking memories of smell, taste and touch as well as sight and sound...' (Nemiroff and Colarusso 1985, p.36).

In one account, a woman in her eighties, after a successful period of individual psychotherapy, met up three years later with the doctor who had treated her. This was after being hospitalized due to a severe stroke. His once 'strikingly appealing patient' had become difficult to manage and the staff could not, or, in their helplessness, would not communicate with her. The result was like a loss of identity. Not only was she out of touch with her personal history, but it was unavailable to others. So her therapist set about reassembling her biography. He used scrapbooks, photographs, news clippings and other personal items to portray her character to the staff. This resulted in far more engagement, both verbal and non-verbal, between staff and patient. Knowing her history made it possible to understand a bit more of her disjointed speech (Cohen 1985, pp.202–203). It strikes me that there is a lesson to be learnt here in inviting far more cooperation between relatives and carers when the old and demented have to be hospitalized and placed in residential care.

For use in the process of psychotherapy, the deliberate 'Life Review' may seem to some of us too directive, but we will probably find the 'naturally occurring process' unfolding easily without being asked for in those patients likely to benefit from analytic work. Straight autobiography is unlikely, but, since the setting is timeless, the patient will be a child one minute and perhaps very old the next. It is the future that is hard to talk about and we need to examine the very strong defences that we all of us, therapists as well as patients, put in the way of looking too far ahead. But that belongs to another chapter.

My oldest patient (of whom more later) was an artist and her paintings were her memorabilia. She wondered whether to give one last exhibition and sell them all for the benefit of 'Help the Aged', but each one reminded her of a precious part of herself and helped her failing memory. At the end of therapy, I accepted an invitation to visit her studio. Without this, she felt I would never truly share the treasures of her inner world. With every painting, and she had many styles, I would say that this old lady 'reinvented' versions of herself.

Viewed from outside, and especially by a younger generation, the old may seem to show us nothing but loss. No wonder many would prefer not to look. 'Old so-and-so is losing his mind.' Is he? And how can anyone judge? The brain cells may be deteriorating and functioning more slowly. The owner of this brain may be finding it harder to use it in order to keep up with the language of his juniors, but the owner of the brain is *not the brain*. In a well-known essay, Winnicott asks why 'the head should be the place inside which the mind tends to be localized by the individual' (Winnicott 1949, p.247). He plays with the words 'mind', psyche' and 'self', defining psyche as 'The imaginative elaboration of somatic parts, feelings and functions, that is of physical aliveness' (Ibid., p.244). The psyche is not seen as inhabiting the brain, but in healthy interplay with the whole body, '…the live body, with its limits, and with an inside and outside, is felt by the individual to form the core for the imaginative self' (Ibid., p.254). In old age, we become increasingly aware of the body's limits, but the mind may not be confined within them. Perhaps we are able to say with St Paul, that even though 'our outward man perish, yet the inward man is renewed day by day' (2 Corinthians 4.16). Winnicott's preoccupation is with the infantile need for 'continuity of being'. Mine is for continuity of being in the late stages of life. If the experience of continuity has been impeded in childhood, it is obvious that we will not hang on to it, when we reach old age. It is interesting how often Winnicott seems to speak to the old, and indeed to any age, quite as much as to the mothers and babies with whom we tend to associate him.

As we get older and fall out of love with our bodies, shocked by the mirror image and frustrated by that faulty edifice of nerve and tissue which no longer functions in lively response to our will, it seems to me important that we should be able to move, however mysteriously, into a new dimension of self, or 'Self', no longer so dependent on bodily sensation or even conscious awareness.

Ageing is like adolescence in that we undergo quite radical, physical changes. During these transitions, it is unlikely that we can just *be* and not examine, with some curiosity, what is happening to us. When in physical pain, our bodies may absorb us entirely. One might say, 'I hurt, therefore I am.' And, if the pain gets agonizing, there may be a longing to end this 'I-am-ness'. At other times, the ageing body, with its creaking joints and slow reactions, becomes quite alien, as though our real selves, still lively and desiring, belong somewhere else.

Old people may get together to discuss both their own and other people's illnesses. Narcissistic as this behaviour undoubtedly is, and self-indulgent and morbid as it may appear to the young, there can be an urgent need to affirm a changing aliveness. By comparing notes, people may be helped in accustoming themselves and each other to bodies which are new and difficult to recognize.

Again, viewed from outside, there may come a time when other people say, 'Poor so-and-so, she isn't herself any more,' or 'He's just a vegetable.' One may be tempted to agree, but that would be to stick to a narrow definition of self, as, for instance, the tip of the iceberg, with which consciousness is often compared. Faced with dementia, I think we need more than ever to respect the sufferer, both for what she (or he) once was, and also for what she, mysteriously, still is, as well as what she may become.

That old lady in the geriatric ward, who droops in her chair, pulls faces, mutters to herself and wets her knickers, has very likely forgotten who she is, but that does not mean that she is not.

On average, I suppose we spend at least a third of our lives unconscious rather than conscious. Every night, in sleep, we sink into a timeless, spaceless state, without logic or grammar, but we are not dead. It is curious that even those who believe in a life after the body's death have so little respect for life in a demented body. In fact, we know as little about the former as the latter.

Jung has this to say:

> Only consciousness of our narrow confinement in the self forms a link
> to the limitlessness of the unconscious. In such awareness, we experience
> ourselves concurrently limited and eternal, as both the one and the other.
> In knowing ourselves to be unique in our personal combination – that
> is ultimately limited – we possess also the capacity for becoming
> conscious of the infinite. As far as we can discern, the sole purpose of
> human existence is to kindle a light in the darkness of being. It may even
> be assumed that just as the unconscious affects us, so the increase in our
> consciousness affects the unconscious. (Jung 1963, p.357)

He also says: 'There is little hope of ever being able to reach even an approximate
consciousness of the self, since however much we may make conscious there
will always exist an indeterminate and indeterminable amount of unconscious
material which belongs to the totality of the self' (Jung 1953).

We are used to thinking of beginnings and endings, a birth and a death of
consciousness with the whole of life laid out in a straight line between. But, if
we could step outside linear time, as we do in dreams, we might be able to think
in terms of depth (though that is also a metaphor) and of being drawn into a
centre of being where conscious and unconscious meet.

CHAPTER 4

Is Sex Allowed?

Plato, in his *Republic*, describes how Sophocles, as an aged poet, was asked about love: 'Are you still capable of it?' Sophocles' reply was, 'To my great delight I have escaped from it and feel as if I had escaped a frantic and savage master.' Plato goes on to reflect, 'Unquestionably old age brings us profound repose and freedom from this and other passions…it is like being delivered from a multitude of furious masters.' But, realistically, he admits that this freedom is not automatic but depends on individual characters and the possession of 'well-regulated minds and easy tempers' (Plato 1908, p.3–4).

Dipping through history, one finds that not all old men are 'well-regulated', nor do they want to be. Take, for instance, Louis XIV, who, at a late age, married Madame de Maintenon. In a letter to her confessor came the desperate plea that 'it tired her very much to make love to him twice a day and asked whether she was obliged to do so. The confessor wrote and put the question to his Bishop, who, of course, replied that as a wife she must submit' (Mitford 1960, p.174). She was 75 at the time and the king 70. But we also hear of much younger women with impotent old husbands. It seems hard to get the balance right, and, at both extremes, the woman seems to have been given no choice but to submit.

In our own century, there has been a sexual revolution, 'rather late for me', said Philip Larkin of 1963, even though he was not much over 40 at the time. People now in their seventies and eighties were not brought up in the atmosphere of freedom that the next generation, at least in Europe and North America, is now beginning to take for granted. Those who were children between the two world wars were, in many ways a 'between' generation, caught, as though in a time warp, of overlapping cultures, the Victorianism of their parents very much influencing an adolescence in which secrecy still prevailed, along with adherence to the Ten Commandments and warnings that masturbation would result in madness if the temptation was not resisted. Rules were, of course, broken, the secrecy sometimes intensifying the excitement of illicit affairs. Girls risked discovery as 'a fate worse than death', contraceptive devices were difficult for them to obtain and abortions were done dangerously in back streets. Adopted children were seldom told about their origins, it being considered better for them not to know. Illegitimacy was carefully hidden.

A patient, who is having psychotherapy in his mid seventies, was brought up with two fathers. 'Daddy One' lived with his mother. 'Daddy Two' lived separately with a housekeeper. The patient spent most of the time with 'Daddy Two', though it was 'Daddy One' who gave him his name. In his adolescence, he began asking questions. The only answer was that he should look at his birth certificate, which he would find 'in order'. When he married, he was 'no good at sex'. Now, as a widower, in spite of loneliness, he feels relief at not having to be sexual. His life has been punctuated by panic attacks and fear of anything he feels unable to control. Not surprisingly, he has a shaky sense of identity.

For the 'between' generation, puberty tended to come a few years later than is usual now. There was no 'sex education' and the facts of life had to be picked up or guessed at, exciting because they were secrets, but often distorted. A sudden sexual encounter in the teens might have felt like what we think of now as child abuse. Those who grew up slowly without the early sexual experiences of so many teenagers today, may perhaps be ageing slowly and are not now so post-sexual as younger people sometimes assume.

It seems that, in every generation, sons and daughters prefer not to think of their parents as sexual beings. This may have something to do with Oedipal feelings and the universal fear of incest, but it may also be culturally determined. There have always been pictures and poems depicting youth, beauty and love, but now, more than ever before, television brings the ideal closer. There is little or no taboo about sexuality in most of its forms, only the unspoken proviso that, in order not to offend aesthetic taste, lovers on stage and screen need to be young, healthy and pleasing to the eye, that is to a conditioned eye that only responds to a collectively approved standard of beauty. If the bedroom is to be opened to the public, it must be given cosmetic treatment to make it acceptable. So one taboo remains. If we allow older people to be sexual they must keep their activities secret. History seems to have come full circle. Those who had to hide from their parents have now to hide from their children.

Couples, still married, retain varying amounts of libido. It is often assumed that, having no menopause, the male sex has the monopoly. The truth may be that ageing men, fearful of impotence, take to boasting about their virility. In other cases, either the husband or the wife has had enough and wants to move on to a post-sexual stage, but it is unlikely that both will feel this at the same time. Not all ageing wives have Madame de Maintenon's problem. Often it is the other way round and it is the wife rather than the husband who wants more than he is physically able to give. The menopause, however it may have been seen in popular myth, is not the end of sexuality. 'Change of Life' is a more appropriate description and, after this change, there is often a renewal of strength and energy, which may pose a threat to ageing husbands.

A couple, whose marriage was not about to break up, asked for marital counselling because they no longer had intercourse. The husband was over 70, the wife nearly ten years younger. She wondered what she could do with her sexuality. He had learnt early in life to hide his feelings. This resulted in a lack of communication. Sexually, the emphasis was on orgasm, his not hers. If he could no longer perform, he saw no point in cuddling or tenderness or even talking about his loss of potency. What they had never discovered was intimacy, a sharing of joys and sorrows which included the disabilities and fears of growing old.

If ageing can be seen as growth into new experience, older men and women may be able to break away from their youthful performances and expectations. If the emphasis is still on macho men keeping their erections, penetrative sex and orgasm, there is bound to be disappointment. Instead of giving the mechanics of sex such importance, I suggest a more hopeful view would be to regard sexual behaviour as a means towards intimacy rather than an end in itself. If men can relax and throw off the need to prove their virility, and if women can accept their bodies, however wrinkled or sagging, as appropriate to the stage of life they have reached, perhaps just being naked together (both actually and psychologically) and accepting each other with freedom to explore new and polymorphous ways of touching and playing, may result in an experience of greater intimacy than when the demand was for mutual perform-ance and/or submission.

To quote Betty Friedan:

> Woman or man, what we all need is some new way to touch, know, love each other the way we really are now, which is not for any of us the same as when we were twenty, thirty, forty. Surely there is something else to be known and felt and said about love in age – yes, love that gets beyond the insoluble dilemmas of the male/female imbalance, the youth obsession, the pressures and terrors of penetration, impotence, the measure of Kinsey and Masters and Johnson, the rages and jealousies that tortured our youthful and middle-aged sex. The fantasies and dreams of youth cannot sustain us or satisfy us in age. Maybe new possibilities of intimacy have to evolve beyond the ways of our youth – inside or outside the old forms of marriage, friendship, family, community – if they are to nourish us in age. (Friedan 1993, p.215)

I react to this optimistic view as one woman to another and I wonder – could a man have written it? Then I think of the many elderly English women who are still virgins at 70, and how difficult for them to face their feelings with such transatlantic openness, and yet surely there must be *some* equally buttoned-up American spinsters! Michael Balint, writing exactly 60 years earlier, made no mention either of intimacy or love. He wrote of old men throwing off conformity by showing a heightened interest in pornography, voyeurism, exhibitionism, homosexuality and fetishism. 'In old age, in the same way as in adolescence, perversions play a greater part than in the prime of life. The transition is perhaps always by way of masturbation which once more assumes great importance' (Balint 1933, pp.69–85). When Balint wrote this passage, masturbation, even though indulged in by most children and many adults, was officially taboo and therefore a shameful secret. It is hardly surprising that remnants of that shame persist, throwing a shadow over a private bit of play that hurts no one but may give comfort and a sense of well-being to people who no longer experience touching and being touched by anyone but themselves.

If sexual fantasies persist, there may be a need to focus on an idealized figure, but not necessarily with the intention of coming physically close or even getting better acquainted. I am reminded of a retired social worker who found himself following a teenage boy through the streets, and how watching was enough. Any notion of acting out his fantasies seemed to him not only irresponsible but absurd. Thomas Mann, in his *Death in Venice* describes such an obsession of an ageing man, Aschenbach, with the beautiful boy, Tadzio:

> The sight of this living figure, virginally pure and austere, with dripping locks, beautiful as a tender young god, emerging from the depth of the sea and sky, outrunning the element – it conjured up mythologies, it was like a primeval legend handed down from the beginning of time, of the birth of form, of the origin of the gods. With closed lids Aschenbach listened to this poesy hymning itself silently within him, and anon he thought it was good to be here and stop awhile. (Mann 1971, p.47)

The passion is certainly of the body, but also a source of creativity. 'The sun,' he wrote,

> beguiles our attention from things of the intellect to fix it on things of the sense…the soul for very pleasure forgets its actual state, to cling with doting on the loveliest of all the objects she shines on…it is only through the medium of some corporeal being that it can raise itself again to contemplation of higher things.' (Ibid.)

The lover and the artist are thus united in this 'regressive' homosexual fantasy. Nostalgia is perhaps a more apt word than regression. There must have been a longing not so much to *have* as to *be* that beautiful boy, symbol of the artist's lost youth.

Growing old does not necessarily mean being alone. Women, nowadays, usually live longer than men, so there are more widows than widowers around. Widowers often get married again, sometimes, but not always, to younger women. Others feel more at ease with their own age group with whom they can share similar memories of youth and understand and accept each other's ageing. Getting remarried in one's seventies, and sharing a bed with a new partner, is a courageous venture. One of the few novelists to describe the uncertainty of such an encounter is Gabriel García Márquez:

> It was the first time she had made love in over 20 years and she had been held back by the curiosity concerning how it would feel at her age after so long a respite. But he had not given her time to find out if her body loved him too. It had been hurried and sad… They did not try to make love again until much later, when inspiration came to them without looking for it. They were satisfied with the simple joy of being together. (Marquez 1989, p.340–341)

Reaching a post-sexual phase cannot be made to happen, nor is it a universal experience. It is a change of focus which may come about naturally, but only if, to quote Jung, 'some higher or wider interest appears on the horizon, a new and stronger life urge' (Jung 1929). One may talk of sublimation, or perhaps, more positively, of transformation. But we cannot force ourselves to adopt different attitudes, only to be open and ready for inevitable change. Once we have got through what one might describe as a second adolescence, we may find ourselves at last in a more or less sexless state, much as we did in childhood. One might compare this liberation from the intensity of sexual craving (Plato's 'savage masters') with Freud's latency period, or see it perhaps as a period of androgyny. To some extent, men and women may change roles. A man, dropping his macho image, may become more inward-looking, more intuitive, with quite a new tenderness towards his grandchildren and plenty of time to enter imaginatively into their games. Thus he discovers a neglected aspect of himself, which Jung would have called the anima. A woman, on the other hand, may find herself more assertive, able to speak in public, sit on committees and be seen, no longer in the shadow of her husband, but as a person in her own right. Before 'old old' age brings a return to dependence, the post-retirement years can be some of the most creative, with fewer borrowed opinions and the courage to trust one's own originality.

But no transformations are complete. Without a residue of longing and nostalgia, the old would lose touch with the sexual world of the young, or, worse still, would merely disapprove. There will be times when the old will look enviously at young lovers and wish they could turn the clock back. Memory will always remain a strong link with all that they once felt and did, as well as what must inevitably have changed.

Whether or not we go on feeling sexual even in our eighties and nineties, we do not need permission from our children, or from a therapist, but from our own psyches, to throw off our youthful conformity or aged resignation, and to take the risk of 'reinventing' our selves.

CHAPTER 5

Loss

We live with loss all our lives and working through the experience is central to any course of psychotherapy, culminating in loss of the therapist. But, whereas, in youth, each loss has a compensatory gain, this becomes less true, or anyway less obvious, towards the end of life. I am talking here of the losses that are universal in human development and which may produce varying amounts of trauma in different individuals. We all have to be weaned, to leave home for school and, sooner or later, to lose our parents. Most of us lose our virginity, our innocence and our dependence, and we will have to face the death of friends or spouses. Eventually we have to die. Maturity, and also how we manage to face ageing and diminishment, depends, to a great extent, on how easily, or with how much pain, we have been able to let go of earlier satisfactions in order to move forward to independence and adventure.

Of course no two lives are the same and, for many people, the losses seem far to outweigh the gains, piling on so many layers of trauma that a fledgling self may become stuck or frozen, and, in Winnicott's language, a 'false' or 'caretaker' self protects the 'true' self, which is too inhibited for growth. A person who has lived to please others and to fulfil someone else's expectations may feel truly 'lost' and almost unable to hold on to life when these all-important others are dead. It is reported that many widows and widowers get ill and die in the first year after a partner's death.

Usually, when we think of ageing, bereavement is what comes to mind. Much has been written about how to live through both the shock and the stages of a bereaved person's mourning. Losing the person with whom one has shared most of one's life, often to the extent of feeling 'one flesh', can be experienced agonizingly as a severe amputation, the death of part of oneself. There are many different bereavements and some of them are difficult to mourn. Divorce may be worse than death because memories are spoilt and there is nothing good to internalize. Losing a child must be one of the worst losses, turning parental expectations upside down. Peter Hildebrand, a psychoanalyst with experience of giving brief psychotherapy to older people, both at the Tavistock Clinic and in private practice, is enthusiastic about results, except in the case of parents who lose adult children. He worked for six months with a woman whose son committed suicide at 21. Coming back after his Christmas break (having left his patient with a colleague on call) he learnt that she had killed herself. She was a woman who had had multiple losses, her parents killed by the Nazis and her husband having died 18 months after their marriage. So there was much mourning to be done. He writes:

> It was clear that her son represented her immortality and that with his death I could not offer her hope or any material change in her appalling circumstances…I was prepared to go through the horrors with her if she wished. I had no option but to accept her final choice, and perhaps do her the small service of containing my anger at her destruction of the creative aspects of me and her retaliation for the way life had treated her. (Hildebrand 1985, p.225)

He goes on to describe Freud's profound mourning at the death of one of his grandsons and how much harder this had been to bear than his own painful cancer. Ernest Jones reports Freud as saying, 'This was the secret of my indifference – people call it courage – towards the danger to my own life' (Jones 1957, p.92).

Hildebrand sums up:

> It seems to me that these people, because they can no longer hope to immortalize themselves, throw into relief the problems that face the rest of us – the reality of our own deaths. Through the existence of our children and grandchildren who will be the receptacles for the immortal parts of ourselves, a sort of psychological gene plasm, we hope to live for ever! (Hildebrand 1985, p.227)

He seems to me to be describing a very concrete immortality, even though the word 'psychological' may refer to an inward rather than a material reality. Nevertheless, the idea that we continue only in our genes, which, combined with so many other genes, would, in future generations, have less and less to do with ourselves, is just as lacking in symbolic or imaginative thinking as the quite different belief that heaven is a geographical place to live in and enjoy after death. Those who cannot ultimately give up their children or let them be separate beings, probably failed to let go of their own parents. And what of those who do not have children? Must their deaths be even more final? We cannot, except in symbols, look beyond death. All we can do is concentrate on our present ageing and the challenge to live our last years creatively rather than giving into despair. Above all, we must not burden the younger generation with our own unfinished business.

A strong capacity for love needs a strong sense of self and one cannot be the recipient of another person's love if there is no self to accept, internalize and be enriched by it. How can one give if nothing has first been given? Sometimes we meet old people who, instead of hankering for their lost loves, suffer from never having had any. There is an emptiness in these people that cannot be filled because it never has been. Such people may have appeared independent in youth, simply because there was no one else on whom to lean. Routine work occupied their days as did physical movement and the ability to be 'distracted from distraction by distraction'. Sometimes these people long for death. One of them asked for euthanasia, regarding her depression as terminal. She looked forward eagerly to what her more independent contemporaries most dreaded, that is ending her days in an institution, which, like the nursery, takes away decisions, attends to feeding and physical needs and makes only minimal demands for initiative or cooperation.

Sometimes wanting to die and even attempting suicide can go hand in hand with a fear of death. The fear is so great that death itself seems preferable to having to live with it. These feelings are not peculiar to age. It is popularly thought that children do not fear death because they have no understanding of it and no experience unless, and until, it affects them personally. Even then, they may console themselves with the thought that it only happens to the old and they can postpone thinking about it. But it seems to me that any fear of the unknown goes together with a weak sense of aliveness and that this may well pertain both to the very young and the very old. Insomnia is sometimes said to stem from a child's need to be vigilant, as though having to look out for indefinable bogeys as soon as the lights go out. I remember asking my mother what I should think about before going to sleep. This was partly to delay her goodnight, but also a need to fill the darkness with thoughts, as though my own would not be enough to sustain me through the night. Fear of sleep was fear of letting go of life. I met this fear when I had a dying girl as a patient. Insomnia was said to be a symptom of her illness. She came to me very tired, longing to sleep yet terrified of life slipping away. She told me that she would spend the nights awake but could sometimes sleep in the mornings with someone alive and awake in the room. This was usually her father, who would sit by her bed quietly reading his newspaper. I told her that I was alive and would stay awake for her, whereupon she lay on the couch and instantly went to sleep for 50 minutes.

Winnicott, in his paper 'Fear of Breakdown' (Winnicott 1974), described primitive agonies, which he named as returning to an unintegrated state, falling for ever, loss of psychosomatic collusion, loss of sense of reality and of the capacity to relate to objects. Fear of breakdown was not of something in the future but of something that had already happened, yet had not been experienced because there was no one (no ego) to experience it. How can one remember a time before consciousness? This unexperienced experience would have been that of annihilation. Continuity of being was interrupted in infancy by impingement and by the failure of a facilitating environment.

If this nameless fear of loss (annihilation of self) preoccupies the child, I would suggest that it is never totally resolved and will be felt again in old age when a person's hold on life is weakened. Perhaps, even at this late stage, a facilitating environment – someone in the room who is awake and alive – can mitigate the fear by restoring a sense of life's continuity through the realization that others will go on living, remembering and being enriched by the life that has to be given up.

George Pollock, addressing himself to the American scene, stresses that 'a very crucial element for successful ageing is the ability to mourn prior states of the self.' He describes a 'mourning-liberation process' (Pollock 1988, p.13). This applies, not only to the obvious bereavements that have inevitably to be encountered in old age, but to all sorts of minor disappointments whose mourning may go unnoticed until a sudden crisis reactivates earlier (perhaps only half digested) pain. He suggests that

> people are continuously mourning something that once was, and adapting to what is present. This is an epigenetic process – if it is missed or negotiated poorly at an earlier stage of life, it will be negotiated poorly at a later stage. It is in this area that psychotherapy may play a key role in getting the mourning-liberation process back on track. (Ibid., p.17)

'The goal of psychoanalytic treatment,' he writes, 'is to make more of people available to themselves for present and future creative and satisfying life experiences... Energy is released for new investment in life...' (Ibid., p.21).

Jung, speaking about the second half of life, alerted us to 'loss of soul', meaning a 'severance of relationship with one's individual psychic life'. This condition showed itself by loss of energy, loss of meaning and a diminished sense of personal responsibility. He described a crisis which might act as a spur to individuation – 'the values which the individual lacks, are to be found in the neurosis itself' (Jung 1953, p.61). If symptoms are seen as attempted solutions, it is only when a person realizes that the symptom-solution repeatedly fails to produce the wished-for move towards creativity and meaning, that a turning-point may be reached. In the depth of despair, there is no way further down save by destruction or suicide. The alternative is a struggle towards the light. Late in life, when there have been many partial solutions, symptoms piled on symptoms, this struggle may be made with a sudden determination to make something valuable out of a last chance. Jung also saw loss of soul as a dissolving of individuality in the collective psyche. The paradox about individuation is that we all lose consciousness in the end, but there is all the difference in the world between a conscious surrender, which is an act of faith, and allowing oneself to be swallowed up.

Pollock speaks of new investment in life. But for how long? Facing death may, for the old, become the only realistic goal and the task of the therapist that of helping the patient to accept the end as a natural process, no more to be feared than birth. Death is not part of life in that we cannot describe it while we are alive, nor do the dead, once it has happened, report back on this momentous event. But neither can the foetus describe how it turns into a baby. Birth, though some claim to re-experience it, has no place in our consciousness.

No movement forward, no transformation is possible without letting go of the past. If we cling to people, places, possessions and what we *think* is important about ourselves, there can be no individuation.

A patient, in her fifties, was haunted by imaginary pictures of her childhood home. If she shut her eyes and let her thoughts drift into fantasy, she invariably found herself standing at the front door, looking back at the house, or going inside, down a corridor and away from the street. When she tried to guide her fantasy and move outside, she found her way to an older family house in which people were dressed in the fashion of 1900, the year her father was born. Now, many years after his death, she wishes she had not been afraid of her father and had got to know him better. She has led a fairly fulfilling life but feels she moved away too soon from her parents and from a brother and sister whom she seldom sees. It is as though she finds it hard to let go of the past and complete her mourning, but almost as hard to re-establish roots with the family of her own generation.

There is a saying attributed to Samuel Beckett: 'When you get old, you must learn to discard things because things are going to discard you.' Eventually we must discard everything we know, but, in the meantime, we have to die bit by bit, as though getting rid of unnecessary clutter, to concentrate on whatever it is that we most value – though even that has to go in the end.

CHAPTER 6

Why aren't they Screaming?

For someone who is young and healthy enough to expect long years ahead, it is almost impossible to grasp what it would be like to have to accept a shrinking future in which there will be little further chance of achievement or drama. In his poem, 'The Old Fools', Philip Larkin described, with unconcealed disgust, the 'ash hair, toad hands, prune face dried into lines' of ageing bodies (Larkin 1990, p.196). He could only surmise that somehow these 'fools' were unaware of the nearness of death as 'extinction's alp', for if they had been, it seemed to him obvious that they had every reason to scream. In another poem, 'Aubade', he tells us what it is like to wake at four in the morning and see clearly 'unresting death, a whole day nearer now' (Ibid., p.208). Those of us who have felt this 'special way of being afraid' will hear, in this poem, echoes of a familiar dread.

But, when we meet very old people, we usually protect ourselves by looking in from outside on a scenario that has nothing to do with life as we know it. To ask Larkin's question, 'Why aren't they screaming?' there must be sensitivity and empathic imagination. Without empathy, the young treat the old like children or perhaps they indulge sentimentally in a wishful fantasy of serenity.

I suggest that serenity, like the Garden of Eden, is something we have left behind very early in our lives, perhaps when we were weaned or even when we left the womb. We cannot bear to turn our backs on bliss and so we hope for it in the future. But it is questionable whether there ever was, or will be, a human experience of lasting bliss, and all we can hope for is some sort of intimation, which we wish we could catch hold of and keep for ever. So, is the seeming serenity of old age no more than a defence? And do the young collude with the old in setting it up and keeping it intact?

The old, at their happiest, are sometimes quite restless. What keeps them going is the urge for some kind of accomplishment. They still have enough ambition to set targets and hope to meet them. Serenity is perhaps postponed, and may never arrive, death intervening while another goal still looms ahead. Friends and colleagues often praise those who are able to 'die in harness'.

But jobs successfully completed are not the only goals. There may be reconciliations which are overdue and forgiveness for both the living and the dead, as well as a need to be forgiven. Or the task may be the overcoming of fear in the face of the unknown, the ability to face death, not as a disaster but as an adventure.

There are certain assumptions that dependent children need if they are to feel secure, but which are inappropriate in adult life. According to an American writer on ageing, Roger Gould, these are:

1. We'll always live with our parents and be their child.

2. They'll always be there to help when we can't do something on our own.

3. Their simplified version of our complicated inner reality is correct, as when they turn the light on in our bedroom to prove there are no ghosts.

4. There is no real death or evil in the world. (Gould 1978, p.14)

In childhood, we may be able to postpone unpalatable truths. Death happens to other people, or else it is so far removed in time that it need not be imagined yet. One child, who has now grown old, used to wake in the night, afraid of endless space and endless time. She was also terrified of annihilation, so could see no way out of the trap which seemed to close her in. The fears started when she was six and increased with the threat, and then the reality, of the war, which she knew might kill her before she could discover any meaning in her life. In adolescence, she realized that she would never find an absolute answer to her problem and nor would she ever be able to prove the existence of God. This uncertainty became so intolerable that she managed not to live with it. She was afraid only of a remembered fear which she told herself would have to be faced at some future time when she could, she hoped, develop the strength to cope with it. Moving through her sixties and beyond, she remained calm. Consciously, she avoided nothing. Yet still she postponed thinking about her fear. She certainly did not see herself as serene though some might have thought her so. Most of the time, she was too busy with life to have room for thoughts of death.

When suddenly the fear came again, she was attending a lecture on cosmology and pushing herself as far as thought could reach to grasp the concept of space-time and its enormity. On this occasion, she let herself experience the vertigo and panic that she had spent so much of her life avoiding. It seemed that a moment of truth came and went before repression set in again. But, after that moment, she was not afraid of what she remembered. It had been more exciting than fearful, almost like dying and coming back to life.

It is often a long hard slog to achieve independence but equally hard, at an appropriate age, to surrender it. One admires those determined people who push themselves, through sheer force of will, towards impossible goals and refuse to admit defeat. We should also admire them if they manage at last to surrender their power and allow others to take care of them. Leslie Farber, in his book *The Ways of the Will*, shows us some of the will's limitations, for instance: 'I can will knowledge but not wisdom…meekness but not humility, scrupulosity but not virtue…lust but not love…religiosity but not faith…reading but not understanding' (Farber 1976). I should like to add to this list – resignation but not serenity, and perhaps also – striving but not finding. In Goethe's *Faust*, the angels are eventually able to proclaim, 'For he whose strivings never cease is ours for his redeeming' (p.282). It is Faust's inability to be content with any earthly delight that saves him from the Devil.

Looking at the lives of famous people, one might, for instance expect Mahatma Gandhi to have attained serenity before his violent death. Certainly the austerely simple life-style of his ashram and daily meditation would suggest as much. 'He who moves among the objects of sense with the senses under control, and is free from desire and aversion, he who is thus controlled, attains serenity of mind' (Mehta 1977, p.8). He would have read these words in the *Bhagavadgita*, which he studied every day. They are quoted by one of his biographers, who talked to many apostles before Gandhi's death. 'What better place to search for that serenity,' said one of them, 'than under the pipal tree with Bapu, who was our steady-minded sage?' (Ibid., p.48). Yet there must have been conflict.

> It is now said that he was born holy, that he had a natural bent for fasting. In reality, he was one of the hungriest men I have ever known…actually he was highly sexed. He tried to control his sexual desires… Everything he achieved was achieved through extraordinary self-discipline and renunciation. (Ibid., p.71)

India's independence was achieved but Gandhi's policy of non-violence failed. At 78, he was a disillusioned and disappointed man whose ideals had not caught on in a political world which he could not control.

How often, when people die, they are remembered less for important work well done and more for the friendship and love they inspired. I remember, when my father died, reading letters from colleagues and friends about his gift for friendship and personal integrity, but not so much about his career.

Nowadays, pre-retirement courses are being organized world-wide to meet a perceived need. In an age of redundancies, early retirement and mass unemployment, people need to see that there is life after (or in between) careers, that perhaps being is more important than doing, and that the protestant work ethic is not the only moral principle. A capacity for leisure may sometimes serve us better than workaholism.

This does not necessarily mean that retired people should choose to put their feet up. Life after work may involve a different sort of doing. It is also a task truly to *be*, that is to realize our potentialities, to drop some of the masks with which we protect our different aspects. The saying 'the left hand doesn't know what the right hand is doing' applies to our split-off partial selves which we too easily mistake for the whole.

Individuation is not serenity, even though serenity may be one of its unsought rewards. Jung, after his break with Freud, struggled alone with unconscious forces which threatened to annihilate his ego and bring him to the edge of psychosis. Only by tearing himself away from Freud, as father, only by taking the risk of giving up security to face an unknown future, could he separate from collective, cultural norms and realize his own distinct humanness. Such a goal is a vocation, and, if the calling is strong enough, there can be no contentment without seeing it through... 'Divine discontent' was Faust's salvation and also that of St Augustine, who wrote in that very personal autobiography called the *Confessions*: 'Our hearts are restless till they rest in thee' (Augustine 1945, p.1). If our lives are to have meaning for us, we need some sort of spiritual journey, though there are many languages, religious as well as psychological, to describe the experience. George Herbert, a poet, who, I think, may have been in turns serene and divinely discontented, suggested that God, having bestowed on man all sorts of gifts, denied him the gift of rest, so that 'if goodness lead him not, yet weariness/May toss him to my breast' (Herbert 1934, p.379).

We all have moments of calm, of being satisfied with the present moment without anxiety about past and future. At these moments, we realize that the tangle of events in our lives up till now has shaped the situation in which we find ourselves. In spite of disappointed hopes, love unrequited or prayers not answered, we could not have arrived in any other way at this particular enjoyment. With ageing, we would hope to see less of a tangle and more of a pattern in our lives, but only if we can kiss a 'joy as it flies' without hanging on to it. It is no good expecting steady serenity, but most of us have intimations and can live, for just a moment, in what Blake called 'eternity's sunrise'.

These intimations come to some, perhaps to all of us, when least expected. Wordsworth called them 'Intimations of Immortality', but, more often, I think, we are not sure what it is that is being intimated and need to surrender to the unconscious for guidance. The following passage from Virginia Woolf's diary is more restless than serene, though with hints of both.

> Great excitability and search after something. Great content – almost always enjoying what I'm at, but with constant change of mood. I don't

> think I am ever bored. Yet I have some restless searcher in me. Why is there no discovery in life? Something one can lay one's hands on and say 'this is it'? What is it? And shall I die before I find it?...I have a great and astonishing sense of something there which is 'it' – a sense of my own strangeness. (Woolf 1926, p.62)

She was in her forties. Fifteen years later she committed suicide. This diary entry about her 'own strangeness' could, I suppose, be interpreted as her neurosis (or even psychosis), as her loss of a sense of identity. But it could also be seen as sanity, a sense of more of herself than she could possibly know.

Serenity, restlessness, individuation do not belong to any particular age. After a person has died, we change our focus. Our memories are not confined to the end of the story, for instance, to Virginia Woolf's drowning, but to the whole mixed pattern of paradox and synthesis, certainty and intimation.

The reported dying words of famous men sometimes surprise us. Beethoven, who was deaf to the serenity of his last quartets, was able to affirm, it seems with certainty: 'I shall *hear* in heaven.' Darwin, who lost his religious faith, said, 'I am not in the least afraid to die.' Newton could stand back from himself and speculate:

> I don't know what I may seem to the world. But as to myself I seem to have been only like a boy playing on the seashore and diverting myself now and then finding a smoother pebble or prettier shell than ordinary, whilst the great ocean of truth lay undiscovered before me. (Brewer 1959, pp.316–317)

And this is how Jung, as an old man and close to death, ends his autobiography:

> This is old age and a limitation. Yet there is so much that fills me; plants, animals, clouds, day and night and the eternal in man. The more uncertain I have felt about myself, the more there has grown up in me a feeling of kinship with all things. In fact it seems to me that alienation which so long separated me from the world has been transferred to my inner world, and has revealed to me an unexpected unfamiliarity with myself. (Jung 1963, p.392)

So he too had a sense of his own 'strangeness'.

What is needed at last is both a striving and a letting go, not like Larkin's 'Old Fools' shutting ourselves inside our heads and retreating into the past or into fantasy, but an openness to what is new and surprising. The individuated person has pushed consciousness as far as it can reach and then let it go. Serenity comes when we manage to accept our limits without falling into despair.

PART II

Time out of Time

(In the Consulting Room)

Teach us to care and not to care
Teach us to sit still.

T.S. Eliot, *Ash Wednesday*

CHAPTER 7

Dare we Risk it?

In Part I of this book, I have tried to look at old age from both the outside and, as far as possible, from within. To understand an older person's inner world, one needs to throw oneself forward 20 or 30 years and feel one's way imaginatively into a new way of being. I have done this exercise with students and been pleasurably surprised to hear them looking forward to grandchildren and to the freedom of giving up paid work, taking up hobbies, travelling and doing what they please. On the negative side, they are aware of loss, loneliness and bereavement, of becoming dependent and possibly having to give up their homes and move into a restricted environment.

As I write, I find myself moving from 'they' and 'them' to 'we' and 'us', which means I am becoming increasingly aware of my own ageing and can identify with the people I write about. With this awareness, I would like to move, as it were, from the world 'out there' into the consulting room and into the inner world of the ageing patient who may be seeking psychotherapy.

Psychoanalytic literature, with few exceptions, is centred on early human development, illustrated by infant observation and child therapy, as well as adult regression. Jungians, as well as Freudians, are now sharing ideas on how the infant emerges from unconsciousness to become separate and individual.

Jung is well known to have been interested in the second half of life, and this I have already acknowledged in describing the task of surrendering one's youthful ego in the quest for wholeness. But, delving into Jungian writings, in search of flesh and blood, individuated persons, I have found, so far, an enormous dearth of actual case material describing how this process is seen to happen in ageing individuals. We have, of course, the important experience of the great man himself, who had to do his own analysis without professional help, but we long sometimes to hear about the struggles of more ordinary mortals and how they may have been helped through the various crises that mark the end of the lifespan.

No wonder therapy with older people feels like exploring a new country into which not many of us are prepared to venture because there are so few signposts.

Even those who go on working into their seventies and beyond – and ours is not a profession dogged by early retirement – seem to prefer working as 'Wise Old Men' or 'Wise Old Women' with the young, whereas more youthful therapists are realistically cautious about this 'pioneering', especially if discouraged by their older teachers and supervisors.

I hesitate to make assumptions and, in fact, I suspect that more of this work is going on than most of us realize. If this is the case, why do we not hear more about it? What we sometimes pick up is a sense of awe when therapists of 40 are confronted with patients in their sixties. One hears such comments as, 'It feels like analysing my mother.' So, it seems, we are up against the incest taboo. There is something really frightening about the reversal of roles that often comes about. However cosily we may expect to be seen in the transference as sons and daughters, it is often mothers and fathers that patients have lost and are seeking again in us. And can we also take on board the patient's sexual desire, particularly, and not unrealistically, present when ageing men find themselves with female therapists? As with our younger patients, *who* we are in the transference may vary from day to day. In the timelessness of an older person's unconscious, there is constant 'struggling between childhood recollections and the end of existence' (Abraham, Kocher and Goder 1980, p.147– 155). To quote the same authors, 'Genitality and pre-genitality merge together to produce not an amorphous mass but a dialectic exchange far richer than in the young person.' The therapist will of course get caught up in this dialectic exchange, often to the point of feeling overwhelmed by the sheer intensity of what is going on.

Freud's words die hard and we may even find ourselves falling back on what he said as an excuse not to work with older people. '…near or above the fifties the elasticity of mental processes on which the treatment depends, is as a rule lacking…old people are no longer educable' (Freud 1905). He was 49 at the time and lived to be 82, during which period his supposedly 'inelastic' mental processes went through many creative changes in the reshaping of his theories. This lack of elasticity, as already mentioned, is refuted today by geriatric experts.

In describing women, Freud added chauvinism to ageism and came out with the following preposterous statement: 'Her libido has taken up final positions…there are no paths for future development; it is as though the whole process has already run its course and remains thenceforward unsusceptible to influence – as though indeed the difficult development to femininity had exhausted the possibilities of the person concerned' (Freud 1933, p.169). He was describing a woman of 30!

One has to remember that the above was written in 1933, over 60 years ago, and that Freud, who was already on the way to old age, would have been accustomed, earlier in his life, to seeing many women dying in childbirth and not outliving their husbands as they mostly do today. But, despite our lengthened lifespans, it seems as though some of his legacy remains. The young still hold on to a stereotype of being old, a mixture of the 'Fool' and the 'Senex', one who is alien and cannot possibly understand how it feels to be in the stage of growing up. One wonders who is projecting what on to whom. I was just getting into my fifties, when a rebellious adolescent referred to my childhood and upbringing as 'Victorian'. I reminded her that I had not actually been alive in Victoria's reign. She looked at me rather blankly – 'Oh, weren't you?' Obviously history was not her strong point. I went on to explain that I remembered what it felt like to be young. It was something I had lived through. 'But you,' I said, 'can't possibly know about being old. You haven't been there.' I think it is this not having 'been there' which is at the heart of the reluctance and caution that I am trying to describe. Whatever age we happen to be, we need, I am sure, to approach working with people older than ourselves with both humility and respect. We need to recognize that we have something to learn from them as well as something to give, and we should be prepared to give, if humanly or practically possible, as much or as little as they ask of us. I must add the hope that a similar humility may be shown towards those much younger than ourselves. Yes, we have 'been there' in the sense that we have all been young, but youth *now*, in the context of the last few years of this millennium, can only be experienced by us indirectly through listening and through imaginative understanding.

And here, I think, the Jungian view of transference might be more helpful than the Freudian. Instead of being expected to cope with the therapist's almost total anonymity – and, for the therapist, to have to cope with wearing that anonymous mask – the patient encounters someone who is prepared, at least on an unconscious level, to share his or her deepest experience of being human, so that, from the ensuing mix-up, something new may be born.

Jung himself describes the dream of a lady of over 60, in which he and the patient, as well as the patient's mother and grandmother, were playing with a very special child. 'The old woman says she can hardly believe we have known the child for only six months. I say that it is not so strange because we knew and loved the child long before she was born' (Jung 1946, p.12). The child, he sees, as a symbol of the self, which comes to birth through the transference, but is also 'timeless and existed before any birth' (Ibid.). He expects this sort of dream to emerge when therapist and patient come together in the 'alchemical marriage' which he uses as an allegory of the transference. In the above example, he shows us how this mix-up can happen late in life. Another quote from the same book, describes what occurs between the two people concerned: 'The patient, by bringing an activated unconscious content to bear upon the doctor, constellates the corresponding unconscious material in him... Doctor and patient thus find themselves in a relationship founded on mutual unconsciousness' (Ibid., p.19).

Indeed, as in any therapy, we take a risk and can never be sure what will be brought to birth. But I think there is an intensity with older people which may be dissipated in treating the young, who are likely to have a wider breadth of interests and many more possibilities of new relationships outside the consulting room. The old, especially those who have been bereaved, have fewer outside distractions, and their inner life, particularly that part which is bound up with the therapist in the transference, may take on an almost numinous importance. No wonder we shy away. But, if we can stand the mix-up, we may get a glimpse of something like rebirth. I have, in my own practice, noticed how often my older patients dream of having babies. When this happens, I recognize some nostalgia for the past, but also that the dreams tend to come when the patient is emerging from depression and able to look forward.

It is always encouraging to hear of analytic work with older people, but sometimes disappointing, and even rather surprising, to discover how often this is confined to short-term, focused therapy.

An article appeared in 1986 in the *British Journal of Psychotherapy* entitled 'Brief Psychotherapy for Unresolved Grief – A Clinical Example from Later Life.' The patient, who was 68 years old and had been widowed for 11 months, was referred by a social worker because of her frequent outbursts of weeping. She was given twice-weekly therapy from October to March and seems to have worked through her grief and coped with separation from the therapist within those few months. To quote the last paragraph: 'It appeared that Mary, despite her years, had been able to use the therapeutic experience in a way that facilitated growth and change, so that she was able to enjoy, in later life, an emotional freedom she had not hitherto known' (Hunter 1986, p.195).

Mary's therapy seems to have been a success story. She was seen again a year after the treatment ended and kept the appointment, not out of need, but because she thought it kind of the therapist to invite her. There was no question of rejection by the therapist, there having been an agreement right from the start that 'brief psychotherapy' was what was on offer. The author quotes Bellack and Small (1978) as advocating that this treatment 'may be of particular use to those in later life.' Other practitioners have endorsed this view, notably Hildebrand (1982), who even goes so far as to say that 'older patients do not have time to hang about contemplating their navels.' I should have thought that time was exactly what is easily available when people are retired and getting old. Another assumption seems to be that the old are always short of money. I can see no reason for the average pensioner being any worse off than younger people, many of whom may be unemployed. If poverty is the reason for short-term therapy in free clinics, that is a good enough reason, but has nothing much to do with a person's age.

The article on unresolved grief raises other questions, which worried me when I read it. One was the labelling of a 68-year-old woman as obviously 'old', thus confirming that stereotyping by younger people which automatically puts pensioners into the category of being unproductive and thus – at least implicitly – less deserving of the therapist's time. Even the distinction I made in the first chapter between 'young old' and 'old old' might be seen as bundling individuals together according to some arbitrary figure, although we must all of us be aware of the extraordinarily variable pace at which people get old and how impossible it is to measure ageing according to calendar years. Another assumption made in the article also had to do with time. For how long are the bereaved allowed to weep? Must all tears be dried within a year? And what on earth is 'unresolved grief'? Eleven months seems a remarkably short period for 'getting over' a husband's death.

I am reminded of another widow in her early sixties, who cried for two and a half years before she felt ready to work through her grief with a therapist. It took her another two years to write a poem in which she referred to the 'adolescence' of her grief, admitting that a crocus on the grave was symbolic of a thaw. Up to then, she had remained frozen and half alive, as though a limb had been amputated. She was allowed, and allowed herself, more than six years of analysis in order to discover an independent selfhood.

Despite Freud's gloomy attitude to analysing older people, his colleague, Karl Abraham, as early as 1919, reported success with patients in their fifties. He observed that '...the prognosis in cases at an advanced age is favourable, where the neurosis has set in its full severity only after a long period has elapsed since puberty, and if the patient has enjoyed for several years a sexual attitude approaching the normal and a period of social usefulness...' His caution is understandable if sexual maturity is the only goal of analysis. Fifty would be 'an advanced age' if he agreed with Freud, as he probably did, about the deterioration of mental processes. But he does admit that, in patients lacking the attributes described, 'psychoanalytic theory can fail even if the patient is young' (Abraham 1948).

Long after Abraham, Erikson showed how each developmental phase brings its own challenge and that the way we cope with youth and middle age will influence how we meet old age and death (Erikson 1959). Among modern psychoanalysts, Pearl King has perhaps had the most to say about the 'pressures which seem to operate as sources of anxiety and concern during the second half of the life cycle and which lead some neurotic individuals to seek psychotherapeutic help when they either have managed without it up to that time, or their neurosis has been inadequately or partially helped at a younger age' (King 1980, pp.153–160). She then summarizes these pressures:

1. The fear of the diminution or loss of sexual potency and the impact this would have on relationships.

2. The fear of redundancy or displacement in work roles by younger people and awareness of the possible failure of the effectiveness of their professional skills, linked with the fear that they would not be able to cope with retirement, and would lose their sense of identity and worth when they lost their professional work role.

3. Anxieties arising in marital relationships after children have left home, and parents can no longer use their children to mask problems arising in relationships with each other.

4. The awareness of their own ageing, possible illness and consequent dependence on others, and the anxiety this arouses in them.

5. The inevitability of their own death and the realization that they may not now be able to achieve the goals they set for themselves, and that what they can achieve and enjoy in life may be limited, with consequent feelings of depression and deprivation. (Ibid., pp.153–160)

This summary applies to people of middle age and onward. Some of the anxieties mentioned, particularly about death, may also be present in the young. Certainly, in some form or other, all five fears were recurring themes in the therapy of my oldest patient whom I saw through most of her ninth decade. Since all therapy includes the experience of loss, the points summarized would seem to have a general application.

When first asked if I would take on an octogenarian, I wondered how 'different' this experience would turn out to be and I asked a former supervisor for advice. His words, 'Treat her like anyone else', were reassuring at the time and certainly prevented me from the sort of categorizing that I have been writing about. In the transference, I was not, as I expected, the daughter that the old lady had never had, but more often found myself in a mothering role. For the next seven years I pondered over my supervisor's words and whether he had given me the right advice. I am still pondering.

The differences, as I see them, have not got much to do with the five fears summarized above. The difficulty is the sheer volume of an old person's life-experience. She (or he) has a long story to tell, a jumble of memories, mourning, resentment, a need to forgive and be forgiven and every kind of unfinished business, along with an urgent desire both to repair damage and to give that life-story some meaning while there is still time left to work on it. This urgency makes people work. In Doctor Johnson's famous words, 'when a man knows he is to be hanged in a fortnight it concentrates his mind wonderfully.' What is difficult for the therapist is the amount of time needed for 'working through'. Whereas the old person's memories of childhood are nearly always clear, an occasion as recent as the last session may quickly become blurred. Both therapist and patient need to repeat themselves over and over again. The work cannot be hurried and one needs unlimited patience in tuning one's responses to the old person's mode of being. If interpretations are forgotten, it is no good feeling frustrated, but necessary rather to trust that some crumbs of meaning have been picked up and stored in the patient's unconscious. What I find myself wanting to offer these patients is not a brief, focused therapy over a few months, twice or three times a week, but, on the contrary, a slowing down of the whole process with sessions spaced at weekly intervals and plenty of time for digestion. Dependence on the therapist, as the most important figure in a lonely person's life, is of course a hazard but my suggested spacing of the sessions may at least ensure that the patient can contain herself, and be seen by others to be contained, without total regression. Ending the therapy is the hardest work of all and will be discussed in another chapter.

Michael Fordham, when he was 79, went to see Donald Meltzer for 'once-a-week analysis on the couch' (Fordham 1992, p.142). Meltzer preferred to call this treatment 'supervision'. He seems not to have liked to see himself analysing such a senior practitioner. Fordham had not wanted to consult a member of his own society, the Society of Analytical Psychology. He also had the notion that he might benefit from some Kleinian input, which he did. Meltzer suggested to him that he write his autobiography, a project 'that has been therapeutic and has helped me accommodate myself to growing old' (Ibid.).

In answering the question, 'Dare we risk it?' we need, above all, to face that

> the real task and goal of analytical work with old people cannot be to readjust them to life, especially to an efficient and productive one, but is most certainly to help them gradually to detach themselves from life and to cover without traumas, the archetypal path of life which is the path towards death. (Zoha 1983, p.51)

In facing such a goal with our patients, it goes without saying, that we confront the inevitability of our own deaths. It may be that working with people who we presume to be nearer to death than we are ourselves, will help us in this daunting task. If not, perhaps we are right in deciding not to risk it, but I hope that more of us in the future will be brave enough not to deny old people, who have the time and money, the same right to that long-term therapeutic experience which we readily give to their juniors.

CHAPTER 8

Regressing

To regress does not mean to relapse, that is to fall back into illness or sin, even though our dictionaries sometimes tend to use one word to define the other. Regression, both in and out of psychotherapy, alternates naturally with progression, and this is more noticeable in older people, and perhaps also in children, than in young adults.

The term is not confined to psychological jargon. A seventeenth-century quotation, gleaned from the 1979 *Oxford English Dictionary*, reads: 'It is necessary that after we have surveyed many objects, we should make a regress into ourselves.' (Montague 1656, p.2470) Indeed, how else can we remember our earlier versions of selfhood and keep a sense of continuing existence? Earlier in our own century, C.S. Lewis, updating Bunyan, wrote of the pilgrim's 'regress'. The straight road through life followed the roundness of the world and brought the traveller back to a visionary island, glimpsed, but far out of reach, in childhood. The way forward was a return journey. We often talk of the 'life cycle' without attending to the implications of returning to the place whence we started. 'Second childhood' has become a derogatory term, a state to be pitied or dreaded. Erikson takes a positive view: 'If at the end the life cycle turns back on its beginnings, so that the very old become again like children, the question is whether the return is to a childlikeness seasoned with wisdom or (and when) to a finite childishness' (Erikson 1981, pp.11–61).

With this last quote, we are up against extremes, that precarious wisdom, which the old can sometimes manage to achieve, and the despair which is its opposite. A massive regression in our elderly patients may indeed seem to us like despair if we see no way out of it. This 'regress into ourselves' looks like firmly bolting the door on the known world, a world which, to the younger therapist, is, as yet, very partially explored. From the therapist's viewpoint, there may be a restlessness, a feeling of irritation, as if even a temporary withdrawal by the older person bodes the finality of death.

Balint's two categories, 'benign' and 'malignant', are helpful, as is Leder-mann's 'stagnation', in showing us whether a particular regression is purely negative, at best a defence, or regenerative, leading to transformation (Balint 1968, p.145; Ledermann 1991, pp.483–504).

The word 'stagnation' suggests a quagmire, 'a very miry place', which Bunyan called 'The Slough of Despond', where, heavily burdened, his hero floundered hopelessly, until Help (personified as a strong man) 'drew him out, and set him on firm ground, and bid him go his way' (Bunyan 1678, pp.12–14). Most of us, both old and young, must have felt something of this paralysing stagnation. To quote Ledermann: 'By stagnation I mean a condition in which a patient's development has remained severely arrested for a long time. In my view this damage usually occurs in the first year of life…' (Ledermann 1991, p.483). In Jungian terminology, what has not been able to develop is the patient's inner child, that urge in every human being to realize himself. The child archetype has never become activated.

> Such a patient – frequently over a long period of time – is unable to regress or progress. I have even come across patients who after years of analytic work, knew about this internal stagnation intellectually only but could not reach it emotionally. In stagnated patients this damaged part is very deceptively covered over by compliant pseudo-adult behaviour. (Ibid., p.489)

She goes on to remind us of Winnicott's false self, hiding a person's true core, and also of how, according to Fordham, the early processes of deintegration/re-integration become stunted.

Patients who get through most of their lives with this, as it were, 'manufac-tured' self, may be totally unaware of what is lacking. To an older generation, psychotherapeutic help was not readily at hand. If known even to exist, it would have been considered as treatment for the obviously neurotic or perhaps only for the young. 'Help', as personified by Bunyan, was of course available in terms of forgiveness for sin. Many older people have been brought up to think of themselves as 'miserable sinners', in whom, according to *The Book of Common Prayer*, 'there is no health', and yet their state of stagnation has not been removed by conforming to 'Mother Church' any more than to their own authoritarian parents. In fact both can be dehumanizing archetypes and if, at last, these patients reach the consulting room, their presenting symptoms tend to be vague – 'nothing really wrong – I don't know what I'm looking for, or whether it's worth wasting your time'. They are often only mildly depressed, discontented with themselves and can see no meaning in life.

And yet, there can be degrees of awareness. Ledermann talks about knowing intellectually but without emotion. It is in fact remarkable just how much a person can know and still be stuck fast in this stagnated state.

Laura had two analyses during her fifties and sixties, with a seven-year gap in between. Her male analyst challenged a helpless, victimized part of her personality, and she became gradually more assertive. When she left him, she still had a husband to lean on. She had always regarded marriage as maturity and separation from her parents. Only when her husband died, did she begin to realize how much she had substituted one prop for another. The marriage had been truly enriching and the mourning took a long time. She went to her second (female) analyst in a considerable state of anguish and became more dependent than ever. What happened over the next few years was a fruitful regression, in which she reached more than assertiveness, realizing at last her hidden potential as a creative person. The discovery was not entirely a surprise. As a child, she had kept diaries and filled exercise books with drawings and words. These were all marked 'secret' in capital letters, and a present she remembers welcoming as a special favourite was a five-year diary with its own lock and key. Some secrets she could never even put on paper but locked away just as tightly in her inner world. It was not so much a question of forgetting as hoarding and hiding. She often dreamed of setting these treasures free, which she did, bit by bit, in her marriage, but always with the fear that what she hoarded would not be good enough to let loose on the world.

The puzzle was why should someone coming from what everyone, including herself, regarded as a stable home with loving parents, have let herself get so stagnated, and why, although she knew herself to be floundering in this slough, was she so afraid to climb out of it. In infancy, she idealized her parents. They were gods and she could not admit that they ever did anything wrong. Sometimes they were absent and there were occasions when they returned to her as strangers. 'I've seen that person you call Mother,' a comment announced to her grandfather when she was two, became a joke. No one recognized – least of all herself – the anger that must have gone with it. During her second analysis, she went on a trip to Eastern Europe. The further she travelled, the more isolated she felt from her analyst and eventually could not remember her face. Back on the couch, she described this sudden blank and was asked if she had ever experienced the same with her mother. She admitted at once that she had, but, until the link was made, had forgotten that she had forgotten. No feelings accompanied the earlier memory. This time there had been confusion and a controlled panic. Her analyst had replaced the mother as all-loving, all-good but not always there.

Eventually her gods had to fail and she was able, not without considerable reluctance and pain, to accept human fallibility. Her later years became filled with goals, most of them realistic, even though time was running out and she still had to learn what limitations accompanied her strengths. Feelings of grandiosity surprised her so much that she was able to laugh at herself but also to enjoy some long-lost fantasies, hidden away since childhood. This lifetime of compliance had never been complete. In a family, convinced of the rightness of its shibboleths, she had been regarded, just now and then, as a bit of a black sheep.

Laura's first analyst used to say that full maturity was only possible after both parents had died. This patient, in her late sixties, had to lose parents and husband and eventually the analytic couch as maternal lap. Perhaps her new-found childlikeness was part of her maturation, as was also, having gone through anger and hate and not a little disillusion, the more tender love that she now began to feel for her ordinary human parents, no longer confounded with archetypal figures. In this case, we see stagnation, regression and some hint of a hard-won maturity. But no case history is a fairy-tale with a happy ending. The life just described is still incomplete and there may be many more obstacles or sloughs of despond to negotiate.

For others, it is very hard indeed to help them get unstuck. If really deprived in infancy, the defences that have been built up are of the do-it-yourself variety. The child has to be its own mother. Subsequently, the patient tends to be his/her own therapist. In the case of a patient whom I will call Barbara, her mother had been ill almost from the beginning of her daughter's life, having a stroke when the child was nine and dying during her adolescence. Thus the daughter had had to be, not only her own mother, but her mother's mother as well. The other family members were male, a father and an older brother. No one helped with the onset of menstruation and she literally did not know what to wear or how to dispose of the sanitary towels when she eventually found out where to buy them. Her father came across them in the bin and told her they were disgusting, implying that she too was disgusting. This was in the 1930s. Yet when she was 16, he sat her on his knee and said her mother would never really be dead if she were with him. So she felt that she carried inside herself a handicapped and 'mad' mother, whom she still had to look after like a damaged child. Her do-it-yourself existence often broke down. She longed to let herself be cared for, yet somehow managed to make a mess even of being the regressed child. Psychotherapy or analysis had become a way of life long before she reached my couch. She was by this time in her sixties and, as though continuing to repeat the family pattern, all but one of her previous therapists had been men. Not long before I came on the scene, she was referred to a woman who warned her that she intended to retire so was unable to give her time for the regression that Barbara felt she needed to experience. With all her therapists, there seemed to be a demand to grow up quickly. She felt bowed down by the weight of other people's illnesses, their expectations of her as nurturer and her guilt, as well as her anger, at not responding to them in the way they wished. She would go to bed, or have a bath, when she wanted a safe place between sessions. With me, as she made clear at our first meeting, she hoped to be held, both metaphorically and actually, but she also wanted her therapy to be fun. Up till now, she had experienced her therapists as making her do serious work and only addressing her adult self, whereas, she now hoped to resurrect the child who had never been allowed to play. She was asking me to invite regression, yet was afraid that, on letting go of her coping mechanisms, she would find nothing inside her, only emptiness. 'Perhaps I'm just a dried-up old woman'. My answer to this was, 'I think you also feel very young and you want to be allowed a lot of time both to play and to grow up slowly.'

My timetable only allowed three sessions a week on consecutive days. This was agreed but she also expressed panic about the rest of the week. I invited her to use the telephone, which she did at specified times and always with the proviso that, although I would be there for her if I could, she had to run the risk of my sometimes being out or otherwise occupied. She wanted a lot of reassurance from me that I could survive her exploration of the deepest part of herself. Or was she being foolhardy? I replied that perhaps we both needed to be a little bit foolhardy – a remark that she never forgot.

In the transference, she relied on me to stay intact as a healthy maternal figure, who, unlike the dying mother of her childhood, would not be destroyed by her energetic demands. I felt reasonably confident in that I had coped in the past with regressed and needy patients and even fairly well with transference love when it turned to hate. So what was different?

In my innocence and inexperience, I had not reckoned with the power of the countertransference. Here was an older woman – or at least older in years – with quite a 'presence'. Her personality filled the room. She was unpredictable and sometimes overwhelming. She knew this and was anxious about how she might affect other people. She would describe herself as a 'bull in a china shop' and sometimes she made me feel very small. Emotionally, it was hard to respond to her child self in a powerful woman's body. Looking back, I realize that I experienced the same discomfort and incongruity that I remember on seeing Dennis Potter's play *Blue Remembered Hills*, in which the children's parts are acted by adults, and how this results in seeing childhood stripped of its sweet and charming veneer so that all its greediness and aggression is laid bare. Barbara's needy child self spoke to my own infantile needs and roused in me primitive feelings which I did not fully understand and which I felt would hurt her if I let them show, so they became unusable. I had enough compassion and genuine warmth towards her to overcome the embarrassment that I now think both of us often felt and which sometimes made us clumsy with each other. My own clumsiness I found hard to admit and defended myself (unconsciously) against it. I was not myself in therapy at this time, nor, except now and then, was the case supervised. For the first year, I was strong enough to endure and also to enjoy what it was like being with Barbara, but that depended on my personal life being more stable than hers.

When my husband suddenly became terminally ill and died two months after diagnosis, I was open with Barbara, as I was with my other patients. Although I have no doubt of her intended concern for me, her own anxiety and sense of loss was far more catastrophic than I had anticipated. She telephoned me on the day of his death and was prepared to let me go. With hindsight, that might have been a wise decision. As it was, I stayed calm and told her I would be taking three weeks off before resuming work as usual. But I underestimated Barbara's infantile terror which left her little room to feel adult sympathy. I also underestimated my own vulnerability. When she flung herself on my couch, sobbing uncontrollably, I remembered how, as an infant, she had been left alone to cry, and, keenly aware of my desertion of her, I interpreted along those lines. She rounded on me in fury at my insensitivity in interrupting her tears which she had at last allowed to flow. Couldn't I see how hard it had been for her to control her agony for the weeks that I had been away? (Long afterwards, she said it would have helped her if I had cried too. I said that would not have helped *me*. What I meant was that I could not have risked getting so much out of control.) She also wanted to get up and dance to celebrate what felt to her like my 'homecoming'. I said that I would rather talk about how she felt. I think I may have referred to any actual dancing as 'acting out' – anything to stop it happening!

Barbara stayed with me for seven years and experienced further bereavements of her own, but I think that what was lost after the impingement of my personal tragedy was never sufficiently resurrected to allow the safe and fruitful regression for which she had hoped. I joined the ranks of those for whom she had had to care. Thereafter I became the needy child/mother of her past. In this confusion of roles, it was difficult, perhaps for both of us, to keep our heads above water, often a stagnant water, unmoving and not good to taste.

Having read Margaret Little's account of her own regression with Winnicott, I realize how much more honest he was than I could ever manage to be about his countertransference feelings, and 'his capacity to stand paradox and ambivalence, knowing them to be inherent in life itself, without seeking ways around, defences against, or avoidance of them' (Little 1990, p.116). His patient was able to survive his having two heart attacks; he survived her smashing one of his valuable possessions. There was an ease and freedom in their analyst/patient relationship and a flexibility about boundaries, all of which I was too anxious to be able to achieve with Barbara. But – I am not Winnicott!

The value of regression to dependence, says Margaret Little, is that it is a means 'by which areas where psychotic anxieties predominate can be explored, early experience uncovered and underlying delusional ideas recognised and resolved via the transference/countertransference partnership of analyst and analysand, in both positive and negative phases' (Ibid., p.83).

I remember how Barbara said to me more than once, 'I don't think you realize how ill I am.' I, along with her other therapists, may have avoided knowing the worst and, as a result, she had to continue her DIY treatment, which so often made me feel left out and that her view of what was happening was so different from mine that we were pursuing parallel lines with no meeting-point.

Inevitably I let her down and felt let down myself. Her decision to end came suddenly; she thought she had been working towards it, but that too must have been DIY because I was not aware of it. The notes of our last session, which was just before another desertion due to my summer holiday, give every sign of her needing therapy, and acknowledging that need, for a long time to come. She broke off treatment on the telephone and refused another meeting, thus avoiding the finality of a planned last session. She had a replacement lined up, with whom I had no contact – I was never told her name – nor do I know whether Barbara was able to regress in more safety than I had been able to provide, and to discover some point from which she could begin to grow.

I wonder if Barbara's story fits with Balint's concept of a 'malignant' regression, that is, to use his words, 'regression aimed at gratification', whereas his 'benign' regression is aimed at 'recognition' (Balint 1968, p.141). I am not really happy in applying the word 'malignant' to Barbara, although she did sometimes show a child's urgency (even greediness) in wanting to feel better *now*. But this impatience had more to do with being old than with being young.

What Freud seems to have overlooked and Balint strongly emphasized, is that all regression inside the consulting room occurs in an interpersonal relationship. There has to be a mix-up between therapist and patient – mostly at the unconscious level – which involves dangers for each participant. After using the image of stagnant water in connection with Barbara, I reopened *The Basic Fault* and came across these words: '…regression for the sake of recognition presupposes an environment that accepts and consents to sustain and carry the patient like the earth or water sustains and carries a man who entrusts his weight to them…without water it is impossible to swim, without earth impossible to move on' (Ibid., p.145).

For a time, I think, I had managed to carry her, either with the buoyancy of living water or the solidity of earth. Getting into a quagmire had something to do with my inability to meet her conflicting demands that I should both 'hold' her and 'do' something. I thought I was being patient but that may have felt to her like complacency. Where she was concerned, 'time's winged chariot' was certainly hurrying near. She was getting old; this was her last chance. There was a desperation about her therapy. This time it had to work. Paradoxically, progress frightened her. Coming out of the regression (and literally letting go of my hand for I had not put an absolute taboo on physical touching) would be to face the reality of ageing and ending. Most of her therapies so far had been abruptly broken off and another saviour searched for and found. Sadly, she repeated this pattern. The more gratification I gave her, the more she craved. It was hard for her to look beyond therapy for therapy had become her way of life.

Pearl King, describing older patients, writes that they 'develop a negative therapeutic reaction which is linked with the fantasy that by avoiding change or therapeutic improvement, they will be out of time and therefore avoid ageing and death' (King 1980, pp.153–160). If this was true of Barbara – and I think there was a hint of it – there was no conscious avoidance.

Regression can become malignant whenever the patient demands that the therapist replaces, rather than symbolizes, the actual mother who was either deficient or dead. Regression, in such cases, is a defence against realistic mourning. Once the loss can be accepted as irreparable, the therapist's empathic recognition can sustain that person (metaphorically) either to swim, or dive deeper into the waters of the unconscious. Jung, although often warning us of the dangers of being so overwhelmed by the archetypes as to risk psychosis, also had something to say about stagnation and the need for movement. In referring to the struggle to consolidate our consciousness and to 'erect barriers against the dark rising flood of the unconscious and its enticement to regression', he stressed that 'this praiseworthy and apparently unavoidable battle with the years leads to stagnation and desiccation of soul... The source of the water of life seeps away... The mind shies away but life wants to flow down into the depth (Jung 1956, p.356). This has to be a willing enterprise.

> No one should deny the danger of the descent but it *can* be risked. No one *need* risk it but it is certain that some will. And let those who go down the sunset way do so with open eyes, for it is a sacrifice which daunts even the gods. Yet every descent is followed by an ascent; the vanishing shapes are shaped anew, and a truth is valid in the end only if it suffers change and bears witness to new images... (Ibid., p.356)

Jung's language is dramatic and reflects his own shattering experiences when he battled alone with the forces of his unconscious. But he makes a good case for benign regression. His downward plunge is also a return – to the mother and to the child archetype, symbolic of rebirth. 'By serving as means of expression as bridges and pointers, symbols help to prevent the libido from getting stuck in the material or corporeality of the mother' (Ibid., p.330). He thus confirms that the therapist can only take on a symbolic role. He goes on to remind us of Nicodemus, faced with the impossibility of an actual return to his mother's womb, and the possibility of being reborn from 'water and spirit' (Ibid., p.331). It is our human capacity for symbol-making which saves us from being overwhelmed.

A natural regression, which need not necessarily have anything to do with therapists and patients, is that backward movement in the very old which enables them to become again like little children and rediscover a childlike capacity for play. Play is symbolic; play is creative; and, in play, we find liberation.

Sometimes it is easy for the old to let go of any rigid controlling of their lives. They have nothing to lose. If they take the step of seeking therapeutic help at a deep level, we should go cautiously and repeatedly ask ourselves whether the regression is benign. Is there movement or stagnation? Or perhaps the question we should be pondering is whether this is something the patient is forcing her/himself to do or is it happening naturally, linking the end with the beginning of life? Jung's warning should be taken seriously. All confrontation with the unconscious is a risky business. Patients without Barbara's experience and know-how about therapy are not likely to hurl themselves into deep water but are more likely to dip in a toe and test the depths. We need to respect the older person's pace which may be slow. In the last chapter, I suggested once-weekly sessions. In this chapter, I have described some of the dangers of more intense therapy. I had not put Barbara in the category of 'the older patient'. Perhaps I was unwise.

Not all regressions are total and some are easily contained in the sessions. I have found my older patients reluctant to use the couch and, in weekly therapy, most of them prefer to face and look at me. But when the transition to the couch can be made, how comforting its cushion and blanket; what a relief, on the purely physical level, to put one's feet up after the hassle of public transport. The quiet, the subdued light, the presence of just one unobtrusive person and the regular return, at a specified time, to an unchanging place; all this is conducive to a feeling of coming home – to the nursery, the mother, perhaps the womb itself – even for one hour a week. And, for the Jungian, there is always that hint of something universal, an assurance of being in touch with the ancestors and the whole history shaping the individuality of whoever it is that now surveys a life soon to complete its cycle. As for age and youth, they are barely distinguishable in the continuing rhythm of regress and progress.

CHAPTER 9

Changing

Changing, becoming different, passing from one state to another, is what all human beings both crave and dread. Every new life begins with a crying baby. There is distress but also affirmation. By that cry, those in attendance recognize that the foetus has become an alive human being who has passed through traumatic change from symbiosis to separation. The process is not without pain, the mother's and probably also the baby's, and yet, paradoxically, we rejoice.

The paradox continues. 'In the midst of life we are in death.' We are born into history, into linear time with its past, present and future, and we cannot stop the clock however hard we try. Both in and out of psychotherapy, a lot of energy goes into resisting.

Older people are not necessarily more resistant than the younger generation. 'She will always be older than I will ever be,' said a man of his female relative who was in her thirties. When she reached 60, she was grey-haired but seemed no less or more mature than formerly. It is often the young who resist, and this applies as much to therapists as to their patients. Before seeking the mysterious 'mutative factor' that brings about psychic change, it seems worth exploring what militates against it; and I should like to discuss the resistance of the young therapist to the older patient.

Children do not expect to change their parents, or, if they should find themselves cherishing such hopes, disillusion usually comes about when they relinquish infantile omnipotence and set out on the lengthy task of separation and individuation.

I remember sitting in front of my 80-year-old patient. She had already had a Freudian analysis with a famous name some 50 years earlier. This was our first encounter. My own mother was alive and not much older. My husband had caught sight of my patient on the doorstep and murmured, 'What a dear old lady.' She was of diminutive size and, when we were both standing, looked up at me with a childish eagerness. Sitting down, she was bolt upright on the edge of her chair, nervous as a schoolgirl. I was immediately confused. She seemed both very old and very young and I felt in danger of losing my bearings. What age was I? I know now that this sudden disorientation saved me from an awed politeness and reluctance to probe into what seemed like parents' secrets. In my own youth, there had been fixed boundaries between generations and there were many areas I would never have been allowed to explore. It was my patient's agelessness that broke through my resistance.

It is important to have a sense of history, not only to place our patients in the social context in which they grew up but also to place ourselves at what ever age we are, so that we can recognize our own prejudices and preferences. I began this book with a repudiation of 'ageism' and of a bias in psychotherapy that favours youth. If we look at the history of psychoanalysis, the founding fathers (note that the first generation did not include mothers) took little account of the new-born infant and the crucial importance which we would now give to mothering during the pre-Oedipal phase. Neither Anna Freud nor Melanie Klein were medically trained, living as they did at a time when female doctors were still thin on the ground. Analysing young children had not hitherto been regarded as essential and somehow got relegated to the women, who became the pioneers both of child analysis and in the widening of developmental concepts affecting adult life. Winnicott knew as much about mothering as any of the women and his intensive contact with mothers and babies, both as paediatrician and analyst, gave him an authority not to be denied. It is interesting that Jung began by believing that children's problems could best be addressed by analysing their mothers, and it was not till the middle of the twentieth century that Fordham's concepts of childhood indi- viduation – and indeed a series of appropriate individuations at different ages – became acceptable ways of looking at the changing patterns of human life. These developmental theories brought about a rift between London and Zurich which was probably as painful for the analysts on each side as the earlier conflict between Freud and Jung. The analytic neglect of early human experience seems to me to be a reflection of how those children, who may become our older patients, have been brought up, *not* to individuate but to fit in with a collective stereotype. 'Honouring' fathers and mothers, very often, meant distancing themselves from intimacy with flesh and blood, fallible parents, so that the archetypal father sternly dominated and expected to be obeyed, and the great mother was assumed to be all-loving (perhaps devouring) and omnipresent, even when the actual mother was quite plainly absent, if not physically, at least mentally, from anything other than the stereotyped children of her expecta- tions.

With history in mind, the young therapist must be open to catch all sorts of nuances both of rigidity and flexibility. The 'between' generation, mentioned in a previous chapter, has witnessed the more or less stable world of its childhood crumble and disappear. In the early years of this century, class distinctions were firmly fixed. A 78-year-old woman came into therapy and found that she could at last get in touch with her anger at having been for most of her life trapped 'in service', at the beck and call of those taken for granted to be her superiors. Neither she nor they had questioned their right to occupy a position handed down to them at birth. 'The rich man in his castle, the poor man at his gate, God made them high or lowly, and ordered their estate.' This verse has now been dropped from Cecil Frances Alexander's well-known hymn 'All Things Bright and Beautiful', but our grandparents would have sung it unthinkingly. It is not surprising that remnants of prejudice still lurk in older people's consciousness, and, even more, in their unconsciousness, although the now diminishing upper classes tend to become embarrassed and apologetic about their blinkered upbringings. What I find more surprising is how so many of them have adapted to such a rapidly changing world.

The Church was one of the frameworks in which numbers of people were enclosed, often without question. It was not only, as it has been through the centuries, the repository of religious tradition, but also an important social structure in which everyone knew his place. Priests and pastors could sometimes be sought out by individuals needing help, rather as one might seek out a therapist today, but the authority of the clergy, bolstered by the power of God himself, could not easily be questioned. Problems were too often seen as sins and the only solution penitence and absolution. So one was locked in a 'take it or leave it' structure. With Mother Church and a patriarchal God, it was hardly possible to advance and become fully adult. Those who broke away often did so with such extreme anger that a bit of projected resentment persists into old age. Others, less locked in, have simply drifted. They may still attend occasional services, perhaps to sing well-known hymns, or for the beauty of the words, only to find that the words have been changed.

With our patients therefore, we need to be sensitive both to each one's unique history and the universal 'Spirit of the Age' to which all of them in childhood belonged, and to which they still unconsciously adhere. It is useful if we are in touch, not only with our own childhood recollections, but our family history, and this entails listening intently to the older people still alive in our families, as well as careful listening to our patients in order to pick up these older people's language. And one must not make assumptions, such as not talking about sex. These patients are old but that does not rob them of their experience. Often they are not so easily shocked as the younger generation expects. But the way they express themselves may be different and possibly (though by no means always) less direct.

Despite a mass of material, much of it jumbled, not everything will be remembered and more reconstruction may be needed than with younger patients. Kenneth Lambert, in his book *Analysis, Repair and Individuation*, sums up our need for a sense of history so that we can pick up 'memories, bits of

behaviour and clues that arise out of their transferences' (Lambert 1981, p.113).
And we also need to be interested in

> whether patients have been brought up within a family or society where
> strong religious and cultural forces attempt to mould children in a
> pattern-imposing way, or whether they grew up in a permissive but caring
> or permissive and neglectful environment, or according to some other
> pattern of child rearing. More specifically, consideration might be given
> to whether they were brought up in the days of Truby King, Benjamin
> Spock or some other fashionable system, or whether indeed their mothers
> in particular, but also their fathers, were reasonably instinctual people
> who could remember both the positive and negative aspects of their
> childhood and so feel their way into meeting enough of their children's
> real needs. (Ibid., p.113)

In Lambert's sensitivity to history, he also *cuts through* history and reminds us
that no generalizations are absolute. Whatever the fashion, religion or cultural
norm, there will always be instinctual mothers (and fathers) who respond
naturally and lovingly to their children, thereby giving them a 'good enough'
start in life. It is of paramount importance therefore that we listen, without
prejudice, to our older patients. They may be old-fashioned or they may startle
us with their modernity. Ageing, as we must constantly remind ourselves, does
not depend very much on chronology.

Our sense of history must be relevant. Today's grandparents were not born
in the nineteenth century and will not present themselves in the same way as
Freud's young hysterics, nor will we behave to them as did both Freud and
Jung, who saw so much of their job as educating their patients. It has been
suggested that conversion hysteria still exists, but with quite a different
manifestation. It is now the therapist who may take on symptoms belonging
to the patient. 'The primary difference is that in the past the hysteric converted
psychic content into a numbed object that was part of *her* body, whereas now
it is the analyst who suffers the effect of hysterical conversion' (Bollas 1987,
p.96). This is an example of projective identification, whereby not only paralysis
but also the patient's pain, both mental and physical, is handed over to the
therapist to share and perhaps to dilute in order to give it back in a more
manageable form. If we can do this without resistance, acting like the 'good-
enough' mother who is in tune with her baby, the result is bound to be, in some
way, mutative.

It would be easy to digress from what is specific to older patients. I would
however like to stress just how much somatic pain one is likely to come up
against and that it is not easy for the therapist to disentangle physical illnesses,
that we may expect in older people, from psychic pain. We should always be
on our guard against expecting medical complications and thus stereotyping

the over-sixties. Making excuses is another resistance which may lead us to do supportive rather than analytical work, even though the patient is all set to tackle the 'real thing'. If all that is wanted is sympathy and a listening ear, professional help, and charging fees, may not be the best option.

A lot has been written about the resistance of patients, much less about our own counter-resistance. Greenson, in his detailed study of psychoanalytic technique, calls our attention to the 'what', the 'why' and the 'how' of resistance (Greenson 1974, p.107). Looking at ourselves, it should not be difficult to see *what* we, as analysts and therapists, resist, both generally in our reluctance to treat older people at all, and also, more specifically, *what* makes us uncomfortable in the presence of a particular patient. We may find ourselves wanting to help who ever that person is to live more fully and to pursue the same life-enhancing goals that we hope to realize ourselves. But, inevitably, that person's life is diminishing and the ultimate goal will be that of facing death. What we resist looking at in our patients is likely to be what we resist in ourselves. As for *why*, our uneasiness and our own admitted, or unadmitted, fear of the unknown, all our unresolved relationships with parental and authoritative figures, our determination not to look too far into our futures, even our denial of the universality of death – all these may blind us to facing what is there in front of us in the consulting room. In looking at *how* we fail to cope, we may easily succumb to temptations to reassure or to change the subject. We may even jolly the patients along and behave as though there is all the time in the world in front of us. Alternatively, we may set a very strict time limit (as many do) and focus on a few selected issues, which happen to be those that *we* feel adequate to confront. Often our patients are braver and know their strengths and limitations better than we do. We would do well to let them guide us into sharing that sense of urgency which has brought them to seek our help, and to realize that they may be struggling with their last and most meaningful crisis, while they still have time and energy to make some sense of it.

When I went into analysis for the second time (and I was not young), I was confronted at the end of my first session with the simple question, 'What is it you want?' I had been a practising psychotherapist for several years and had been taught by my various mentors not to ask questions that tied the patient down to having to give an answer, but rather to slide round the various issues with comments such as, 'I wonder if...' or, 'it seems to me that...' But, when challenged so directly, the jolt of having to find an answer (and I did not see refusal as a choice) was salutary. My most spontaneous response would probably have been an anguished cry of 'Help!' But spontaneity was lacking in that first session and I produced a lucid answer, which, in fact, remained valid through all the hundreds of subsequent sessions. I was only too aware of change, mostly in the form of loss. Externally, my life was getting different, my body was ageing. There was nothing I felt like denying. I desired, most of all, to cope with what I saw as inevitable change and to find some appropriate, but still creative, way of living the rest of my life. I have no doubt that I was helped, but how? What was the mysterious mutative factor that, without any promise of solution, nevertheless brought about enough transformation to feel better about facing each day with a gleam of hope that it might bring newness rather than dreary repetition?

> There is still an ultimate question, much less easily solved than the riddle of the Sphinx, as to what the mutative factor is, where it is to be found and how it can be activated. (Hubback 1988, p.204)

Looking at psychoanalytic theory Strachey wrote a paper back in 1934 which seemed to give an answer (Strachey 1934). What he had to say made such an impact on his contemporary analysts and those who came after him that it was reprinted in the *International Journal of Psychoanalysis* more than 30 years later, in 1969. Etchegoyen, in his paper 'Fifty Years after the Mutative Interpretation', evaluates Strachey's thinking: '…the word mutative means something that changes the psychological structure – just as a genetic mutation changes the cellular structure' (Etchegoyen 1983, p.449). Strachey concentrated on the reality of the present moment and the consulting room as the only place where change could come about. In Kleinian fashion, he described the patient's behaviour as being like that of a young child, caught in the vicious circle of projection, introjection and reprojection. The analyst, in his neutral setting, could make a breach in the circle by acting as an *auxiliary superego*, which differed from the patient's original, sadistic superego in being impartial rather than involved in the conflict. Through what Strachey described as *mutative interpretations*, the patient 'introjects a different object, and in doing so the internal world (superego) and also the external world changes since his next projection will also be more realistic, less distorted' (Ibid., p.449). Strachey thought it important that the patient should become conscious of two things – an instinctive impulse and an object that does not tally with that impulse, by which he must have meant an analyst who gives a new response. He spelt out a clear message that *only* transference interpretations could bring about change.

In the context of the anonymous analyst sitting behind the couch and responding to the patient's free associations by transferential interpretations and nothing else, it is perhaps surprising to read that the analyst emerges from the process as *a real figure*, while, at the same time, the only way to ensure the patient's ability to distinguish reality from fantasy is to *withhold* reality as much as possible. The paradox is tantalizing.

We would probably agree that external reality, other than what the patients have introjected and made their own, and, most especially, that reality which belongs exclusively to the analyst or therapist, is an irrelevance and, except in very small doses, likely to confuse rather than enlighten. But if, as I have already argued, once-a-week therapy (quite probably in a chair rather than on the couch) is more suitable for the really old than a classical analysis, I find myself questioning how much of Strachey's theory is applicable to that sort of work, except, of course, as a discipline to pull the therapist back from unhelpful, untherapeutic (or even self-indulgent) digression, in order to face the reality of what is happening between the two people concerned.

Whatever style we adopt as therapists, I think we would also agree that it is important to speak the truth, even though we may often doubt the factual correctness of our interpretations. What matters, and what may even bring about some change, is whatever accords with the patient's subjective truth, and that happens whenever there is such understanding between two people that each offers the other his own version of truth without dogma, or even certainty, but always open to question and fallibility. This honesty and open-mindedness may result in something like Balint's 'harmonious, interpenetrating mix-up' or we may think in terms such as Jung's 'alchemical marriage', this being the image he used to symbolize transference/countertransference; a marriage that neccessitates 'genuine participation, going right beyond professional routine' (Jung 1946, p.35), the mingling and eventual transformation of both participants, the therapist emerging as the 'wounded healer'. Whereas Strachey, in his formal language, recommended certain techniques to bring about change and had nothing (except perhaps implicitly) to say about countertransference, which, if recognized in his day, would have been seen as a drawback, Jung invited an active involvement that would seem to have some of the characteristics of a love affair.

Falling in love can, of course, be illusory, even psychotic, and certainly transferential. If, as professionals, we dare to use the word at all, we might appropriately think of it in the way that St Paul, in his famous Epistle to the Corinthians, writes of 'charity' (at least as translated in the Authorized Version, which may incidentally be the one familiar to our older patients). And we need to be clear that this usage does not imply, as in its distorted meaning, a duty to the underprivileged, but the kind of love that we are able to give spontaneously, and for as long as necessary, to people whom we respect. 'Charity suffers long and is kind...is not puffed up...rejoiceth in the truth...'

If analysis, or psychotherapy, is undertaken in the spirit of a loving relationship, which has a beginning and end, one, or both, of the two people concerned will have to suffer bereavement. The ending will be by mutual agreement but the ultimate decision belongs to the patient, who, provided things have gone reasonably well, feels changed enough no longer to need the analyst/lover. When the patient leaves, it should perhaps be an occasion for satisfaction if the therapist feels the more bereaved of the two. 'Charity...seeketh not its own...'

Both Kenneth Lambert and Rosemary Gordon have written about what Lambert calls the 'Agape Factor'. Agape (translated in the Authorized Version as 'charity'), lies behind the analyst's ability to listen to the patient as a real person. 'This skill is not necessarily exercised through techniques like screening, keeping silent etc. It may operate within dialogue just as well' (Lambert 1981, p.41). A decade later, Gordon takes up the theme. Agape she defines in terms of sympathy, friendship and mutual respect. But it is the passion of Eros that pushes us beyond ourselves. She believes there is

> a real need for Eros, whose dynamic force must complement and counterbalance Agape... Where not just 'normality' is sought, but actual transformation and individuation, there the transporting power of Eros must come into play and be available. Thus, so I believe, Agape and Eros are both essential constituents of an analyst's experience and love for his patient. (Gordon 1993, pp.249–250)

Still the mutative factor remains elusive. How do people, in or out of love, manage to change each other? Judith Hubback (quoted on p.68) sees the possibility of change as lying in the self, and, to her, this means the Jungian self, rather than Freud's structure of id, ego and superego. In her case material, she shows how two selves, that of the analyst and that of the patient, affect and change each other, moving 'from the possible to the actual when two selves meet... We take part in change, it is integral to us as alive and active human beings' (Hubback 1988, p.204).

Instead of attempting to answer the Sphinx's riddle, it would, I think, be more fruitful to describe some meetings of selves. In doing so, I hope to examine the nature of reality in therapeutic sessions and show some intermingling of transferential and ordinary human relating. Even with full permission, there is always the difficulty of exposing what a patient might prefer to keep secret, so I proceed with care, as well as with gratitude and respect. In each case, the patient is well into the second half of life. Children, if any, have left home. Retirement either looms or has had to be faced. Being alone is what the future is seen to offer. Being with someone in the sessions may be a rare opportunity for intimacy. Transference, whether positive or negative, is likely to be intensified.

It took Tony 70 years to integrate the shadow of being Jewish. His family had changed its name. His features did not betray him. He had been brought up as a baptized Christian and had a public school education. Distant relatives, whom he had never known, disappeared in the Holocaust. He had fought in the Second World War and deplored Hitler's final solution as much as anyone, but he had never let it touch him personally. He had a successful career and random love affairs, but he was afraid of getting close to any human being. He never married, lived on his own and, despite his many acquaintances, was beginning to fear the emptiness of old age. He had been an only child, his parents were now dead and he had not kept in touch with other family members, so he could now keep his secret without fear of being found out. But he could not control his dreams, which became increasingly repellent as he grew older, and he would wake up choking as if saved in the nick of time from the gas chamber. Also in dreams, and only in dreams, he felt all the guilt so common to Holocaust survivors.

He was secretive about coming into therapy and would park his car in a distant street, continuing furtively on foot and looking over his shoulder to make sure that no one recognized him. Even the sight of another patient made him shake with fear. He chose a therapist with a Jewish name. Now that he was desperate to 'confess', he felt that he could only do this with someone who was 'tainted' with the same 'evil', and at first his manner towards her was both offhand and conspiratorial. When the moment came for his great confession, she showed no surprise but admitted, quite honestly, that she was not herself Jewish, though happy to be married to a Jew and take his name. At first he did not believe her; she must be pretending, just as he had done all his life. He stormed out and missed the next session. She wrote, assuring him that she had told the truth and showed compassion that he should have suffered years of unnecessary guilt. She also admired his courage in seeking help at last. He was persuaded to come back and they speculated about long-forgotten incidents of anti-Semitism, which seemed to have driven him in early childhood to such an extreme attempt to change his identity. In her countertransference, she felt some of the guilt of the Jew who has survived, even though, in her case, survival would not have been in question. She also felt irrational guilt for *not* being Jewish.

There followed a lot of weeping for the fuller life he might have allowed himself and he mourned, most of all, the rootedness in family and descendants which had been so important to the ancestors whom he repudiated. He felt that it was too late now for the begetting of children as the only immortality that made sense to him. The nightmares stopped and he experienced a lightness in letting go of his years of secrecy.

Apart from the all-important decision to start therapy, the outcome depended on the chance factor that his 'Jewish' therapist was not what she seemed, and she could even understand something of his feeling of being an outsider through her own experience of marrying outside her familiar milieu and identifying with a persecuted race. It was important to him that she was genuinely not a Jew (and therefore not to be despised) and yet totally accepting of his Jewish identity. In the transference, she had shared his shadow, but it was her positive reality that brought about transformation. His therapist had an unusual opportunity to facilitate change in the patient's 'self'. This holds good whether we think about the Winnicottian 'false self', whether we focus on early narcissistic wounds, or embark on a Jungian search for individuation. If a strict rule of 'transference only' had been maintained and the patient left with his fantasy, the whole course of therapy would have been different and there is no way of knowing the result. In this case, the therapist did not trust herself to proceed convincingly on a false basis, nor did she feel like misleading her patient into accepting a distortion of her own important reality.

An 80-year-old widow, whom I will call Ruth, resolved to talk about facing death but dialogue about it with her therapist always petered out. On the other hand, talking about an experience is not the same as *having* the experience. Even the fear, which had often been intense when alone in her room at night, would, when she came to her sessions, be only a remembered fear, something to talk about when the panic was over. She regarded her therapist as her lifeline and therapy had to do with living. She used to say, 'I want you to be there when I die,' but sometimes that could be modified to the more realistic hope that her therapist would be 'there' somewhere in the world, alive and perhaps able to visit, write, or, at least, be affected by her death. An aspect of her strong desire to be in charge of what went on around her was that she hated the thought of the world continuing when she had gone.

One experience of death was brought into the consulting room. She described her sister's funeral and that she had suddenly become cold and felt pressure on her head while standing with her son in the crematorium. He had put his arm round her to give comfort, which was unusual in that he did not easily show his affection for her through touching. Relating this incident in therapy brought back the coldness and pressure. She turned pale and looked as though she were going to faint. Her therapist had strong feelings of wanting to touch her. Instead, she said what she found it difficult to say. 'I think you experienced the coldness of death and the pressure was as if you, yourself, were in your sister's coffin.' The old lady nodded. The therapist brought her a glass of water and the colour came back to her face. Touching the patient's cold hand with her own warm one, as she handed the glass, was the only physical contact they ever had. It was not that this therapist had an absolute rule about not touching, although her patient probably thought she had. Resisting this temptation came from a desire not to short-circuit the fear that had shown itself at last. In this session, as in many others, there was plenty of metaphorical touching which undoubtedly they both recognized. When the patient had gone, the therapist felt lonely and cold and found herself shivering as she turned up the heat. At that moment she would have welcomed a bit of human touching for herself.

To effect a change in the self which involves accepting the dissolution of that self is perhaps beyond the scope of any therapy. There were intimations now and then of an ability in Ruth to live through, and for, others rather than for herself, but there was also a strong rebellious streak, reminiscent of the adolescent who drove a golf ball through her father's study window. She could not quite shake off the role of caring for people which had been put upon her by her father's exhortations to look after her delicate mother, and, indeed, looking after someone meant that she was the one in charge. But she also yearned for others to give her the same care. Above all, she wanted to be heard and understood. This, her therapist could do for her. The withholding of actual touching had something to do with an awareness of the patient's pride and prickliness. There was quite a conflict between caring and being cared for and no doubt she did not make it easy for her only son to get it right.

Ruth's mother had been put unrealistically on a pedestal, her father criticized for not understanding her and putting restraints on what she wanted to do. Some of this idealization (almost idolization) of mother dissolved in the therapy and brought more appreciation of father and also some identification with his strength. It was the therapist who found herself firmly on the pedestal, and this loving transference was never resolved in the therapy. Instead, the old lady continued to carry an internalized ideal (though not, mercifully, an idol) into her nineties.

Interpretations had to do with physical symptoms, identifying a prickly skin rash as anger, coldness and numbness as fear of death. When her conflicts showed themselves mentally rather than physically, they became more accessible to consciousness and she could work on the emotions produced.

A year after ending therapy, Ruth telephoned and wanted to come back — 'or have we broken the spell?' The therapist said she thought they had, but some contact is maintained and the unspoken boundaries, that seem to have become redefined, are not abused. The occasional contact satisfies the need to know that, as the old lady gets weaker, her therapist is alive and well and has not forgotten her. It is perhaps a comfort that she will live on in the mind of the therapist.

Laura (mentioned earlier) was also widowed. She plunged quickly into an idealizing transference with her female therapist. She was, at the time, living with her very old but still dominating mother. 'You're using me as the all-good parent,' said her therapist, 'and that means making your mother all-bad.' The patient replied that she was quite aware of what she was doing and knew the difference between transference and reality, 'Because,' she said, 'I'm not quite mad.' She found herself pleading, 'but please let me do it.' She was missing a remembered perfection, or so she pictured it, of mutuality, warmth and understanding, which her husband used to provide and which,as a child, she imagined having from her lively and caring mother. Asked what her husband had given her, she murmured, 'Everything.' The therapist looked doubtful. 'Can one really get *everything* from one person?'

She dreamed of being invited to a candle-lit dinner party where her therapist, as hostess, looked on her lovingly while she talked to the guests. It was like being treated as a favoured child who was allowed to play with others while her mother kept careful watch over her. Lying on the couch, she would sometimes shut her eyes, or let her gaze wander round the room and enjoy the pictures and vases of flowers. But it was important, when she turned towards her, that the therapist was looking at her all the time, however much she allowed her own eyes to stray.

In another dream, she ran across a field into the therapist's arms and enjoyed the feel of her silk dress. She herself was wearing something just as silky but of a different colour. In the dream, she was young. Both these dreams were experienced as moments of blissful union, though, in the second, there were reminders of childish games of hide-and-seek and how important it had been both to find and be found. It also linked with memories of the feel of her mother's evening dress when she used to come and kiss her goodnight before going to a party, and of the softness of her skin. But there were other compensatory dreams in which the beloved therapist became large and ugly, with a red face and a loud voice, and was strongly reminiscent of a hated schoolteacher. Towards the end of her therapy, she dreamed more realistically of the two of them, as friends, usually enjoying country walks or visiting places that she was aware they both knew.

The therapist did allow, for quite a long time, the illusion of perfect harmony, but eventually suggested that it would be useful, and perhaps more interesting, to explore differences between them. There was the question of possible rivalry. The patient was openly envious of the therapist's achievements, both known and imagined. 'Have you thought,' she was asked, 'about my envy of you?' Of course not. That she could be envied was unthinkable. Another shock was that, when fantasizing about meeting in a different context, the therapist suddenly remarked, 'But we might not even like each other.'

Separation came slowly and they did not make an ending until the patient was ready to let go. In the last year, she found herself talking frantically against time. Her fantasy was that every problem she had ever had must be solved before it was too late. The only negative bits of the transference were when she realized how much her therapist forgot what she said. It was as though, if forgotten, she would cease to exist, and she could not allow herself a separate existence, partly shared with friends and partly of value only to herself. Her therapist could not strengthen her faith in God and she had to accept that what they had in common was the same kind of uncertainty. She intimated that, when the therapy was over, she might seek a spiritual director. 'I'd like to think,' was the reply, 'that there were some things you could work on by yourself.' After a pause, Laura murmured, 'Thank you for saying that. I would only get hooked on another person.' And then, 'Perhaps I *will* try by myself.'

When at last they finished, the parting was gently managed and not so agonizing as anticipated. Some weeks later, the patient wrote, 'I don't miss the sessions, but I do miss you.' It was a letter to a very good friend.

Sometimes the most mutative things we say are not realized at the time. What broke this patient's repeated pattern was being told that she could not expect 'everything' from any one person. As the youngest child, she had been very much her mother's baby. Early in life, she had learnt how to charm people into petting and spoiling her. But neither her mother nor subsequent adults had always managed to be consistently there. Childhood memories alternated between being blissfully caught up in an atmosphere of love and approval, where everything she did was praised, and being left alone to amuse herself without comfort or understanding. Achievements recognized and applauded by others brought oceanic feelings of bliss, but, in between these peak moments, she felt the need to cling to a series of idealized figures. Getting older brought a dread of fewer achievements and the deaths of people she loved. Eventually she was able to appreciate living on her own as a new phase in her life when in her late sixties and onward she could be able to grow up at last. She was surprised at how much she was enjoying the freedom of no one telling her what to do. There were of course troughs of loneliness, but these were manageable, as long as she had friends to share selected bits, rather than the whole, of her life's experience.

If we think in terms of individuation, all three of the persons described must have been struggling for an optimum development of their potential selves, a becoming of what they always had it in them to be. If this is seen as mere unfolding of a genetic blueprint, we leave out the possibility of conscious choice. We are none of us obliged to realize more of our selves than we are comfortable with, and what Jung called the 'achievement of a greater personality' is bound to involve accepting and integrating all sorts of negative features that we have turned away from or projected on to others. Consciousness of our own wholeness, warts and all, is not an easy choice.

Tony was pushed into accepting his Jewish identity by unconscious shame. The change that he set about making so late in life was hard and painful. Therapeutic help could do no more than get him started on his impressive about-turn. The mutative factor in his therapy had to do with external reality. When he tried to project his shadow on to his therapist, she refused to accept what was not in accordance with her own reality. If she had been as Jewish as her name suggested, her countertransference might either have colluded with his persecutory feelings, or, in a positive way, shown him how to be proud of his 'self'.

Jung never accepted unconsciousness as an excuse. To develop more of oneself, one must, of necessity, increase self-awareness, and that means separating from the collective and taking responsibility for one's own past, present and future. Individuation is never more than a goal and a process. There can be no final achievement, for this would mean stasis, and the human condition is unimaginable without the tension of opposites. Perfection may be desired but it is undoubtedly a mistake to expect it. A patient, not described above, but also over 60, suddenly saw her goal as being able to be 'an imperfect person'. This realization would be at least a partial individuation.

Ruth and Laura were each of them battling with separation and fusion, a coming to terms with what is universal and what is personal. In old age, perhaps we should expect to see less ego and more self, a conscious giving back to nature (or to God) of the separated individuals that we took such pains to become. But this may be too much of a paradox to have much bearing on what actually happens when humans mature and try to grow wise. For those in extreme old age, I even doubt the importance of self-awareness. I have already suggested that life comes full circle and one may, as in infancy, be self and not know it. But an earlier conscious choice will have affected the quality of what each of us contributes to history and to the future.

In the therapeutic encounter, one of the goals we should be able to realize is that of discovering just how many choices are open to us at all stages of life. If human beings can grasp at least a hint of this kind of freedom, they may be better able to seize their individual destinies rather than succumbing blindly to a collective fate.

Change is inevitable. What we do with it depends on a lifetime of learning when to struggle and when to accept.

CHAPTER 10

Remembering and Forgetting

Some words keep coming into my head, even a faint echo of a tune: 'It's easy to remember and so hard to forget.' Or was it the other way round, 'It's so hard to remember and easy to forget'? It makes sense either way but I find myself not sure whether it is a song about remembering or forgetting. Remembering may be burdensome but forgetting is often frightening.

Older people collect painful memories as well as constant reminders both of continuity and discontinuity, whether through possessions, pictures and photographs or by visiting the streets and seeing the houses where they used to live. They get drawn to places that are pain-producing such as the graves of people whom they have loved, but these invoke good feelings as well as bad. Not all nostalgia is painful and a constant revisiting of the past keeps them in touch with their roots.

It is well known that some old people start forgetting people's names. My mother used to refer to Mrs 'Thing'. In fact she knew quite a crowd of Mrs and Mr 'Things', and we used to tease her about the 'Thing' family. We may find ourselves expecting this forgetfulness as a symptom of age, assuming that the young are never absent-minded. Boswell, In his life of Johnson, makes this comment:

> There's a wicked inclination in most people to suppose an old man is decayed in his intellects. If a young or middle-aged man, when leaving a company, does not recollect where he left his hat, it is nothing; but if the same inattention is discovered in an old man, people will shrug up their shoulders and say, 'His memory is going.' (Boswell 1791)

It is probably kindest to face the problem head on. If a person is able to voice fears of increasing forgetfulness, any well-meant attempts at denial are likely to be seen as the evasions that they undoubtedly are. A scholar in his late seventies was told by a kindly doctor that, as he had such a well-stocked mind, there was no room for anything new. Since this was said to him in admiration, he took it as flattery and was pleasantly amused. My oldest patient arrived one day for her session in a great state of agitation. 'I took a taxi,' she gasped, 'But I forgot both your name and address.' All I said was, 'You're here.' I had a feeling that she remembered what really mattered. In childhood she had been called a scatterbrain. Had she minded? 'Not in the least. I had better things to think about.' I suggested that she still remembered those better things. I also acknowledged that her memory was getting worse. Senility was a long way off but she had seen it in her mother and sister and was clearly frightened. I had, without reassurance, to acknowledge this too, but sometimes we were able to joke about the scatterbrain part of herself and the way she left little notes, pinned up on the walls, all over her flat, so that she could be reminded, in whatever room she happened to be, of her engagements and any jobs she needed to do. As long as she could find ways of coping, she felt at ease with herself but always with an anxiety, sometimes amounting to terror, that these devices would eventually break down. She knew that I could not take this fear away but she wanted it recognized. And this recognition – even when I felt helpless about not giving her more, and had moods of hopelessness regarding her future – was of therapeutic value in that it made her feel understood and cared for in the all-important present moment.

We often notice that the very old, who have forgotten what happened yesterday, remember events of their childhood with great clarity. We are impressed, sometimes awed, by a wealth of everyday detail which, to younger people, is the stuff of history. What is good to remember is retained and it can be returned to like turning the pages of a favourite book. But memory is selective and sometimes it is a shock to go back to a once-known place and see what seems like a separate reality from that which impressed our younger selves and which we have cherished over the years. As the details fade, others are no doubt added from unconscious fantasy, and the resulting 'memory' is an amalgam of inner and outer worlds. In so far as we thereby create our own memories, they become our private property and we may doubt the reality of the scene 'out there', its appropriation by other people and its contamination with fantasies different from our own.

Sometimes the pictures are vivid but the feelings are lost. There is a difference between looking at a mental scrapbook and re-experiencing what it depicts. In 1895, Freud wrote: 'Recollecting without affect almost invariably produces no result' (Freud and Breuer 1974, p.57).

It is well known that Freud, initially through hypnosis, uncovered early sexual traumas that had resulted in symptoms. Whether what he discovered were incidences of actual sexual abuse or infantile fantasies is a subject provoking considerable discourse today – why did he abandon his seduction theory? Without entering into this particular argument, I have already touched on forgotten trauma, and, in an earlier chapter, mentioned Winnicott's 'Fear of

Breakdown' (1974) as fear of a trauma that has already been lived, but not actually experienced, there being no self (in his language, ego) mature enough to encompass it and make it accessible to memory. I wonder about those who claim, through regression, to re-experience the trauma of birth. Feelings are reported of restriction and suffocation and moving through a dark tunnel towards light and air. Similar reports come from those who nearly die and are resuscitated. These come from mature people whose capacity to remember is in no doubt. It is worth noting that, once they have seen the light at the end of the tunnel, they are seldom afraid of their eventual dying.

Such experiences are sometimes dismissed as being no more to do with what we know about birth than they are evidence of an afterlife. But it is often remarked that watching a person die is like watching a birth and one might do worse than speculate about death joining up with birth in a union of opposites, conscious/unconscious, remembering/forgetting, thus completing a circle. But this is guesswork, perhaps wishful thinking. All we can fruitfully discuss is how forgotten traumas can be re-experienced very much later in life and whether the kind of picture-book memories that I have tried to describe have any lasting or therapeutic value.

The layman is still inclined to view psychoanalysis as the application of a technique to bring back repressed memories and to suppose that the act of remembering a forgotten event is all that is needed to restore peace of mind. Some of Freud's early case studies might seem to confirm this view, though I doubt if many of today's practitioners find their task as simple as that.

Here I would like to introduce Jane, who underwent therapy (for the third time) at the age of 60. In her case, she recovered feelings which could not be attached to a remembered event. It was as though her mental scrapbook was torn in pieces and she could not glue them together. Her previous therapists were both women. She had not allowed herself to stay with either for more than a year. But she paid a lot of attention to her dreams and believed that they had important truths to tell her. She also had a relationship with her unconscious, which was personal and rather like Jung's Number One and Number Two personalities. The dark, unconscious personality seemed to speak to her, both in her dreams and in what she called her 'meditations', which were waking dreams and might, in Jungian language, be called 'active imagination'.

There was some reluctance, but also a feeling of inevitability, in her choice of a male therapist and she was ambivalent about what she called his 'connections with the Church'. After her first session, she dreamed of a man in a black hat. They embraced. No words were spoken but they understood each other. There was a table with a map showing an illuminated path. This started by being straight but, in the middle, turned into a maze, before straightening out again. She knew that her therapist would have to guide her through the maze. The dark man said, 'Feel my back. You can use my strength.'

In a later dream, she was in her therapist's room. She said, 'I will have to leave you because I'm having an affair with another man. I would like to come back when I've sorted it out.' She did not tell him this dream because it seemed to her dismissive. It also aroused uncomfortable sexual feelings which made her wonder why she should bother – 'at my time of life'. Outside the therapy, her marriage was stable and, in general, things were going well. Why, indeed, did she bother?

In her next dream, she found herself in an underground room in the Tower of London. There was a jewel in the centre. Her therapist was standing opposite and they both looked at the jewel. On waking, she said to herself, 'He's seeing it differently,' as though their points of view could not be brought together.

She liked her therapist's comfortable room, with its oriental rugs and abstract paintings, but not the approach to his house. She disliked his dark hall and dreaded entering the door on the left. She told him the sessions were like sandwiches. The good part was in the middle between a bad beginning and a bad end. After the sessions, she wanted to run. When the first session was over and the times fixed for continuing, she had doubts about whether she had done the right thing. Yes, her unconscious told her she had to go back to find her spirit. She knew she needed to see a man and she wondered about problems with her father. After a few months, she said, 'when I come here, it's "unwillingly to school".' School had been a convent. She knew that she had toyed with the idea of becoming a Catholic but was vague about the circumstances. She had visited a priest in his seminary. She wondered why. She had been 16 at the time so these visits should have been easy to remember. In her therapy, she found herself re-experiencing ringing the bell, entering a dark hall, being shown into a room on the left – and meeting a priest!

Anxiety increased. A year into therapy, she had a fantasy of being in a metal frame which was lowered into the sea and moved with the current. Suddenly she entered a whirlpool. The door of the frame was flung open. She needed to hold the frame together; otherwise she would be swamped or torn to pieces. This was one of her 'meditations'. Another was similar. She was in a small boat, carried by the river's current through a deep canyon. Ahead of her was a waterfall. She knew that there was no escape and she would have to go through the 'whirlpool'. She said to her therapist, 'It's like taking a cork out of a bottle.'

Her unconscious was personified as a dark man. He was like an extra therapist. He kept saying to her, 'You must acknowledge the emotion.' She was aware of needing to release pent-up feelings; otherwise they would be somatized. She had suffered a few years before from a debilitating illness which she had never quite understood. She felt now that, as she got older, she would not have enough strength to contain her turbulent feelings. The container was getting thin and a lot of repressed stuff would seep out.

She went though a crisis in her therapy. Outside the sessions, she behaved in a way she did not recognize as belonging to her usual self. It was as though there was a split-off part of her who wept and called on God. She had periods of needing to be by herself. She was half remembering, half reliving something from the past. The dark man, who was her unconscious, kept saying, 'Write it down.' Her husband comforted her without wanting to hear exactly what she was suffering. He knew that she needed affection and he gave it to her. She felt that she could not have gone on with her therapy if her external world had not been in good order. The therapist said, 'You give me the impression of someone whose world has been turned inside out and upside down.'

Months later, she reread everything she had written down. There were violent dreams of nuclear explosions and many references to the number 16.

It was extraordinarily difficult to feel her way back into being 16 and to remember clearly what happened. She knew there was this priest, whom she had to call 'Father', that she visited him in the seminary and went though a door on the left hand side of a dark hall. She also knew that he talked to her about sexual matters. She had always remembered two of his fingers – so clearly that she would still have been able to identify them – and she associated them with sex. There was never any sexual discussion in her family. The priest left the country when she was still in her teens. No one told her whether he was sent away. She had not talked or thought about him for years. Now, in her therapy, she could voice feelings and she cried out, 'I can't get rid of this priest,' and, addressing her therapist, 'You weren't there for me.' She had curiosity and imagined that, if a genie were to offer her just one forgotten memory, she would ask to know why she was sent to visit Father So-and-so in the first place.

She came to a point in her therapy when she was convinced that there had been sexual abuse. Then she had doubts. There was no factual memory to address, only a replay of feelings. Her therapist asked her if she wanted him to acknowledge that it *did* happen. She said it was important that he believed she was being honest when she thought it did. During the time that she was re-experiencing the feelings, she had no doubt of the facts. Now she was left with 'perhaps'. She knew that her uncertainty might be a defence but she also knew that it could not be forcibly removed. When she was going through her 'whirlpool', she had nightmares. If she said it never happened, she was attacked by a woman. If she said it did, her attacker was a man. She interpreted this as being caught between the thinking and feeling parts of herself.

This therapy is still going on, so there is no knowing what further secrets remain to be revealed. Memory is personal and selective and an unreliable guide to factual truth, unless corroborated by additional evidence. But truth itself is personal in that what has meaning for each of us, and what is therapeutic, is the truth that we discover for ourselves, what we feel to be true, rather than what we can prove. Jane may continue to protect herself until a time when (if ever) she can cope with unpalatable facts: or maybe there was no abuse, other than feelings of abuse, and these can be just as traumatic. There are many possibilities, one of them being that what she presented was a screen memory, hiding an earlier trauma, for instance abuse by her actual father, mistaken for the priestly father. But what matters is that she should come through her maze or her whirlpool, scarred but not totally demolished.

Not remembering can result in a variety of behaviours, which are usually described, by Freudians and Jungians alike, as 'acting out'. To quote Laplanche and Pontalis: 'The subject in the grip of his unconscious wishes and fantasies, relives these in the present with a sensation of immediacy which is heightened by his refusal to recognize their source and their repetitive character' (Laplanche and Pontalis 1973, p.4).

This is similar to the Jungian use of the term 'inflation', whereby the unconscious invades consciousness with archetypal material whose symbolic nature is ignored. This should not be confused with healthy enactment, which by acknowledging, not projecting, and not being overcome by the archetype, results in creative rather than compulsive behaviour. Whereas Jane was too overwhelmed by her feelings to get in touch with factual memories, the person who 'acts out' tends to bypass both fact and feeling.

Barbara, whose regression I described in an earlier chapter, exhibited 'acting out' both inside and outside her sessions. She described a weekend during which her husband had not acknowledged her neediness and she had carried her sleeping-bag to and fro between the houses of various friends, searching for a bed where she felt safe to rest. After a session with me, she had been so exhausted and heavy with sleep that I was persuaded to let her lie down for an hour in my waiting-room. Another time, after a regressed session, she had felt like a free child and had bought herself fish and chips and a can of Guinness (described as mother's milk) which she had tried to share with a tramp (an aspect of herself), before lying down to sleep on a traffic island, an 'island of safety', which the busy traffic had to circumvent.

She had a way of erupting into my room, spilling parcels, like pieces of herself, wanting to share with me bags of cherries, books she wanted me to read and a weedy seedling to put in front of my window for light and air, and for me to care for it. In these ways, she made a display of her neglected and messy child self who had to earn attention through gifts and acts. Insights came and went, but linking this exhibitionist behaviour with memories of her deprived childhood was painful, and, in my countertransference, I could feel both hurting and hurt and did not find it easy to be confrontational enough to consider questioning the reasons for her gifts. The plant that she gave me grew and filled the window and even managed one pale flower, though it mysteriously wilted and died soon after she broke off therapy. I may have 'acted' out my own anger by ceasing to water it, though I have no memory of any conscious negligence.

'Acting out' as a substitute for memory must always involve regression as well as being related to the transference. Patients behave on the couch as though they are restless children. In one case, another woman in her sixties wrapped herself in two rugs (thoughtfully provided) and left them in a tumbled mess at the end. Eventually the therapist showed irritation. 'It was like not having to make my bed,' said the patient and folded them carefully after every subsequent session, thereby stealing extra time. This could have been an act, conscious or unconscious, of revenge for her carefully regulated ration of 50 minutes (known as the 'analytic hour').

Other patients come early and make themselves heard in corridors or bathrooms, in one case leaving on a tap and depriving the therapist of hot water. There may be awareness of voices in the consulting room, arousing sibling rivalry or Oedipal feelings of wanting to intrude on parental secrets. Perhaps stamping and splashing were the only sure ways of being heard in childhood, or perhaps the feelings were too intense for a child's vocabulary. Memories are likely to become more accessible if they can be put into words and a verbal interpretation of what is going on may break through the compulsion to repeat. Sometimes this arises from the therapist's memory of stories the patient has recounted. For example, one might find oneself responding to excessive punctuality or early arrival with, 'I remember you used to get good marks for school attendance.' Noises off might be met with, 'Of course you wanted to make your own noise to make up for being shut out of your parents' bedroom.'

But there comes a time when it is too late for interpretations. My oldest patient, already mentioned in this and earlier chapters, is now in her nineties, living in a residential nursing home, a fate that she used to dread. During her seven years' therapy with me, we faced, and even joked about, her failing memory, but on a recent visit I was struck by how my own distress at seeing her in the day room, among other wheelchaired and lost-looking residents, was so much stronger than her own. Recognition of her surroundings comes and goes, but, increasingly, it goes. Her memory loss protects her from fully realizing the helplessness of her situation. When her dignity is attacked, she vigorously brandishes her stick and threatens the staff. So she has been put on tranquillizers, and I have to accept that she is probably happiest in a dreamy state which lets her be in touch with her youth rather than her age. I was warned that her talk would be about people whom I had never met, but, after so many years together, I felt I knew them well. I was happy to collude in (in the sense of playing with) her fantasy of being hostess, and therefore the centre, of a large house-party over which she was also in control, having invited all these guests herself.

One of the most obvious instances of forgetting, which affects all of us part of the time, and some of us all the time, is the loss of our dreams. This forgetting seems no more peculiar to the old than to the young and, in practising psychotherapy, I have found my really old patients giving more attention to their dreams than many of those who are younger, busier, middle-aged or 'young old'. The dreams of old age seem often to resemble those of childhood. My first reported dream, aged seven but recorded in my diary when I was eight, was about an angel of death, and I can remember earlier dreams of being overwhelmed or lost. I met a ten-year-old recently who kept a 'dream book' which she let me read. Her dreams were similar to mine and, in many of them, she was under water. Dreams of drowning, suffocation and loss are not really surprising in those whose ego is weak, whether at the beginning or end of life. As a small child, I had recurring dreams of 'hot stuff' falling on me from the sky. I knew nothing of volcanoes.

My 'old old' patient wrote a dream down for me: 'I was wandering about in that horrible derelict piece of waste land (the usual one) and all around is dust and dirt, nets and curtains, and I'm trying to get out of this, and, when I get through one curtain, there's another one and I can't get out and I'm completely enclosed.' Up to this point she was describing a variation of a dream that had recurred since childhood. This time, feeling depressed and lost in her old age, she added, 'Then I turn to look at myself and – yes, this is my life. I can't get out – marriage, art, child – all has been a failure.'

The waste land in this dream had not always been horrible. It was a remembered place where she and her sister used to play, and it was next to a churchyard. Her sister had been afraid of the graves but she had enjoyed drawing the shapes of the tombstones. There was a low wall, which, in her dreams, became too high to climb or see over, so she was trapped, with no way out. In the pictures she painted, she always saw to it that there was an open gate or a river flowing towards the sea. She did not like the stillness of lakes.

In one of her dreams, she lost her memory. The worst had happened and she knew she had become senile. 'But I can't remember the dream.' Of course. There was nothing to put into words. But the dream experience had been powerful.

The language of senility is similar to the language of dreams in that it is elusive and metaphorical. Images take the place of words. Incontinence is felt in the body as a flood or explosion and it is these that may be spoken about. There is indeed a wall that we cannot climb, nor can we see the other side. Our eyes are not necessarily blind but death is beyond our horizon and may appear as a blank wall. All that can be said is, 'I can't see.'

If something is forgotten that does not mean that it is not experienced. We all dream but we cannot always translate what we dream into words. In fact, the report of the dream is not the dream but only a second-hand copy. There must be pre-verbal dreams and post-verbal dreams, with speech occupying the space between. One who is in the middle of life, can neither remember nor foresee this dreaming, uncontaminated with words, which may be experienced by animals, as well as very young or very old humans. At the end of life, sinking into unconsciousness, the whole of life may become a dream and 'in that sleep of death what dreams may come/When we have shuffled off this mortal coil/Must give us pause…'

So let us pause a moment and think about the importance of both remembering and forgetting.

Gerhardt Adler reminds us that 'forgetting is essential for our sanity – without it we would be suffocated in an infinite ocean of images. There would be no space for new experiences nor for growth based as it is bound to be, on ever renewed conscious choices' (Adler 1979, p.120).

For any achievement, we have to sacrifice memory. Writing this page, now, at this moment, I am, with a deliberate act of the will, forgetting last night's dreams, my next appointment, my plans for the weekend, what to eat, what to wear – the list is endless.

When William Golding tried to describe Neanderthal man, he imagined him struggling to express thoughts: '"I have a picture." He freed a hand and put it on his head as if confining the images that flickered there… His eyes deep in their hollows turned to the people imploring them to share a picture with him' (Golding 1955, pp.15–16).

In order to hang on to this picture, he had to choose from a kaleidoscope of images, which he thought were in his head, and find a way of communicating the one picture which was important for him at that moment. His struggle reminds us of the very young and the very old as they endeavour to pin down just one elusive idea which it is hard for them to put into words. But, in every act of remembering, we need to shut out and forget the quantity of other pictures that crowd upon us. Remembering and forgetting are in opposition to each other and need to be held in a fine balance if we are to live effectively with other human beings in a limited world; a world whose boundaries need respecting if we are to stay within the borders of sanity. On the other side is psychosis and a severance of connection with our friends.

To quote Adler again: 'Remembering and forgetting are such vital manifestations – one could almost say tools – of human existence that without them we would live in a world of chaos. Without remembering we would not be able to recognize any object, person or situation and we would live in an aimless world; without forgetting we would be so swamped and drowned in impressions and images that we would lose our orientation' (Adler 1979, p.119). He goes on to say that 'consciousness is memory and memory consciousness' (Ibid., p.119). But, as a Jungian, he would know that what is conscious is infinitely small in the vast collective from which we come and to which we return. If birth is 'a sleep and a forgetting', so perhaps is death.

CHAPTER 11

Ending

The end of therapy is more often than not referred to as 'termination', presumably because of Freud's well-known paper, 'Analysis, Terminable and Interminable'. This title is Strachey's translation of '*Die Endliche und die Unendliche Analyse*'. So the word has got stuck in psychotherapeutic jargon and we tend to go on using it, despite its negative association with abortion, which would often mean getting rid of something unwanted and best forgotten. Perhaps some endings do turn out to be abortions but we all strive, whether we are therapists or patients, to manage good endings in the same way as we hope for a good death.

I was relieved, on looking through psychoanalytic journals, to find my repugnance spelt out by a Freudian: 'Termination usually refers to something final and irrevocable. We speak of termination of pregnancy…of terminal illness, of railway termini where there is nothing beyond – a final stop… Often it involves a tragedy or a disaster… There is no new life beyond termination of pregnancy' (Pedder 1988, p.495).

In Freud's paper, he was questioning whether there ever could be an end to analysis and he recommended, certainly for those of us who practise it, that we should get ourselves reanalysed every five years.

If we think of therapy as a life within life, it can be seen as a natural development from birth and (by way of regression) infantile dependence, through adolescence, towards separation and (with differing Freudian and Jungian emphases) individuation; after which, most important, and in one's own time, the ability to let go and die. That is the ideal, but 'termination' might be said to occur whenever this natural process comes to an untimely end, either through the patient's unwillingness to move out of regression and perhaps a destructive undoing of any achieved progress; or it may be because of the therapist's inadequacy in getting things unstuck or in losing the will to continue. There are of course unforeseen problems such as illness, unavoidable moving away or even the death of one or other of the people concerned. In therapy, as in life, death may come out of season.

If we examine some of the psychoanalytic guidelines for a patient's readiness to end, those of us working with an older age group are likely to feel unsatisfied. Strengthening the ego and making the unconscious conscious, genital maturity, a capacity to love and to work; these would seem, on the whole, to be the major aims of youth rather than age, and, if these aims are not achieved, they may be realistically mourned when a person gets old, as missed or bungled opportunities. But, after mourning, there should surely be a letting go of yearning and wistfulness and a realization that, towards the end of life, there may be different goals to pursue, different choices and different freedoms.

Winnicott, who was concerned much more with infancy than age, made this wise comment: 'You may cure your patient and not know what it is that makes him or her go on living. It is of first importance for us to acknowledge openly that absence of psychoneurotic illness may be health, but it is not life' (Winnicott 1967, p.117). These lines were preceded by the all-important question, 'What is life about?' Instinctual gratification seemed to him an incomplete answer. A person needs a 'well-established' capacity for 'total experience'. 'It is the self that must precede the self's use of instinct...when one speaks of a man one speaks of him *along with* the summation of his cultural experience. The whole forms a unit' (Ibid., p.120).

In talking of the self, he was not using Jung's language, yet he came close to it and went on to quote Plaut, a Jungian analyst, in describing the human capacity to form and use images, combining them into new patterns, depending on the individual's ability to trust. In Winnicott's words: '... *Trust* in this context, at the time of maximal dependence, before the enjoyment and employment of separation and independence' (Ibid., p.116). I may seem to have strayed from describing the criteria for ending therapy, but Winnicott, through his exploration of cultural space, does succeed in showing us that there is more to life than sexual satisfaction, more even than relationships, important as these are in the building up of trust. That space between mother and child in the earliest stages of their separation, must not be intruded upon either by the mother, or the child's future therapist, if this means robbing that person of a place to play. So, among our criteria, we might add a capacity for play, and this can apply to patients of any age, but perhaps especially to the old, who may have lost, and at last refound, a longed-for freedom and the confidence to use more of their underused creativity before time runs out.

Looking at rather different criteria, we notice that Jung did not expect to succeed in the impossible task of bringing *all* unconscious experience into consciousness, but felt that the gap between conscious and unconscious could be reduced.

> The aim of psychotherapy is therefore to narrow down and eventually abolish the dissociation by integrating the tendencies of the unconscious into the conscious mind. Normally these promptings are realized unconsciously or, as we say, 'instinctively'…All this passes off smoothly and without difficulty provided that his (the patient's) unconsciousness contains certain ideas of a symbolic nature… If, on the other hand, there is a tendency to dissociation, perhaps dating back to youth, then every advance of the unconscious only increases the gap… As a rule outside help is needed to bridge this gap. (Jung 1956, p.442)

We know, from his own confrontation with the unconscious, how close he came to having no gap, but, perhaps because he came through without succumbing to psychosis, he could write fairly optimistically about trusting the unconscious not to get the upper hand. A person is able, one might say, to 'play' with symbols and, like a sane child, to *know* that he is playing, without turning his symbols into concrete facts. We might see the symbols as occupying Winnicott's transitional space, not only that which is created between mother and child, but between our conscious and unconscious ways of being.

When it comes to ending therapy, Jung seems to have believed that this could often come to a natural end in the patient's own time, facilitated by the holding presence of the therapist. Each patient lives according to his own myth. Jung wrote of a 'guiding function' which gained influence over the conscious mind without the patient consciously noticing what was happening (Jung 1953, pp.131–132).

Fordham reports on how Jung, with one of his female patients, admitted to getting things wrong. She came into one of his dreams, which he described to her in the next session. She immediately developed a cluster of psychosomatic symptoms.

> The whole case worried me so much that I told the patient that there was no sense in her coming to see me for treatment. I didn't understand two-thirds of her dreams, to say nothing of her symptoms…I had no notion of how I could help her. She looked at me in astonishment and said: 'But it's going splendidly! It doesn't matter that I don't understand my dreams. I always have the craziest symptoms, but something is happening all the time.' (Jung 1954, p.334)

Fordham tells us that this was her way of showing him 'that his holding frame and his continued existence were far more important than his understanding' (Fordham 1978, p.11). This patient's capacity for playing with symbols was obviously highly developed. Jung had to contain his confusion. He allowed himself to learn from his patient but was able, in time, to relate her symptoms to his own explorations of the collective unconscious. They had work to do together, but it sounds as though this patient was well on her way towards individuation, whether her conscious mind knew it or not. In this case she obviously trusted her unconscious and trusted her therapist.

There is all the difference between being overwhelmed by the unconscious and surrendering to it. At the end of life, there has to be a surrender, but it seems that we need first to be fully conscious of what we are doing, so that even that surrender is, as much as possible, of our own volition. This necessitates a readiness for death, a readiness that cannot be willed, nor can therapy necessarily bring it about, but at least it can be faced – which may be difficult for both therapist and patient – before ending their therapy sessions.

Of crucial importance is the question of transference and its intensity in psychotherapy with old and lonely people. However illusory the patient's attachment may seem to the therapist – and perhaps the therapist would prefer to deny its strength – for the patient this may be the only real relationship in an empty life. And by 'real' I mean that it is not entirely an illusion. Knowing that the therapist continues to be alive and well may have become the only mitigating factor between hope and despair. It is hard to draw any definite line between transference and the alive presence of the therapist whose anonymity is seldom, if ever, complete. The very fact that the first session is used as an assessment on both sides (which, as one of my supervisors used to put it, is for finding out if the therapist/patient couple can bear to be in the same room together for hundreds of hours) – this must mean that what is vaguely referred to as 'chemistry' comes into the decision. Knowing *about* a person is not the same as knowing. A lot of baggage does, undoubtedly, get 'transferred', but also, at an unconscious level, there must be some sort of knowing – one might call it trust – that this is a person one really wants to be with. Accordingly, an alliance is made. It is analogous to marriage (which is also full of projections) and, like marriage, it sometimes fails.

In describing a difficult ending with my oldest patient, I am aware of inviting criticism from those (very sensible) practitioners who advocate short-term and low-intensity therapy for patients who are really old. I can only say that I am not an expert in what is, to my mind, a much more difficult way of practising, and also that, with patients who are clearly asking for more, I would rather follow my senior colleague's initial advice – 'Treat her as you would anyone else.' Looking ahead, this is how I would want to be treated myself, were I to ask for therapy in my eighties, and I would hope not to become a victim of ageism.

This patient had had an analysis many years before so she knew more or less what to expect and was prepared to commit herself open-endedly for as long as we both could manage or thought fruitful. I saw her regularly, once a week, for seven and a half years, ending a month before her eighty-seventh birthday. For the first five years, neither of us, as far as I can remember, mentioned ending. Her GP wrote, 'I am convinced that she needs you more than me, at least for the time being.' This 'time being' was left open and, having reassured me that her physical symptoms were not serious, he never tried to impose on me any opinion of his own about ending.

During our years of therapy, she and I both had to be hospitalized, I lost my husband and she had a series of bereavements, including brother, sister and many women friends. If I had to be away from her, she was afraid I would die. She kept trying to talk about facing death but usually the subject got changed. One day she said it looked as though she would still be in therapy when she was dying. Then she talked about how she hated money and preferred to have nothing to do with it. I wondered if she was saying she would eventually find me too expensive. This was the first hint she gave me that one day we would have to end. Tentatively, she hoped that, even after finishing, I would remember her and come and see her when she was dying. She added, 'But you mustn't die first.' She wanted to look after me, just as she had had to care for her idealized, though invalid, mother. But she was also longing to be cared for herself and this was harder to admit, even though a repeated theme in her therapy was her way of swinging between dependence and independence. She looked after her relations by trying to send them into therapy and, as a fellow artist put it, 'turning her flat into a clinic'. She was opening her studio to those of her friends who enjoyed painting but were old, ill or lonely and needed encouragement. She then got overwhelmed by their demands, even angry, but went on doing it; and she got furious with herself for sleeping in the afternoons. She wanted to be busy and nothing she did was good enough. She said, only half jokingly, that she felt she ought to save the world. She gave me the feeling of time running out and that this had something to do with her fear of not saving her inner world in her therapy. Sure enough, in the next session, she brought up the subject of ending. She gave her reason as self-indulgence and that she ought to save the money for her son and his family. I said to her that I thought we should begin thinking about making a good end. She immediately talked of something else but mentioned the subject again, rather fearfully, just before I was taking a holiday. I suggested we might work towards an ending in a year's time. I also said that being able to end voluntarily might be more satisfying than waiting till she found it physically impossible to make the journey. She had by now given up public transport and had to rely on taxis and friends. Immediately after my holiday, she said crossly that she remembered me talking about ending but could not imagine what I meant. I repeated that I had suggested another year, in which we might look at the end of therapy and also the end of life, and I recognized that this would be hard for both of us.

There seemed a lot still to be resolved, her idealizations, chiefly of her mother, her son and me, her longing all her life for her father's love. I asked myself (and also a colleague), 'Can this therapy ever end?' The answer seemed suddenly clear: 'Not till she can acknowledge her hate.' When she next managed to mention ending, it was with gloomy resignation. 'How can anything change at my time of life?' We recognized together that her outer circumstances were not likely to improve but that there could still be an inner journey. She said she would be all right as long as she went on painting.

It certainly seemed that she was becoming reconciled to ending and we even agreed on a date, but a year seemed a long way off. A month later, she had forgotten the date and, when I reminded her, said pleadingly, 'But you didn't mean it, did you?' She also managed to say, 'I'm using you as something to put in the way of facing death.' This seemed an important moment. Some time afterwards, I came across Pearl King's comment: 'Patients may behave as if they had the same span of time before them that they had in their adolescence, leaving the analyst to carry the urgency of their situation and denying their actual position in the life cycle…and if they can manage not to be part of life, they will not die' (King 1980, pp.153–160).

As we approached the agreed date for finishing, which was also the end of the year, I realized how she dreaded Christmas and got depressed during the dark winter days. We had touched on the end of therapy and the end of life, but we had not worked through her idealized transference. I did not want to be her executioner and it was a relief to both of us when we renegotiated and decided on a date in July before a natural summer break.

I remember a session when she mourned her many losses, husband, parents and, to some extent, her only son whom she had lost by his marriage to another woman. 'Why,' she asked, 'can't I let him go?' This was followed by, 'Why can't I let you go?'

At last we talked about what she had failed to get from her mother – mothering. In adolescence, she had believed her mother to be the only one who understood her needs and who had supported her maturing adult longing for independence. It was her mother who had let her go to art school. But no one had supported her weakness, not even her husband and certainly not her son. She had mothered her own mother, then, in turn, both husband and son. Her weakness could only show itself in physical symptoms. Twice she had found, and idealized, a female therapist. As a result of coming to me every week and getting mothered, her symptoms (tachycardia and a skin rash) were discarded as though no longer necessary. What would happen, I wondered, if she managed to hate as well as love me?

Compassion (and weakness of will) tempted me to postpone the ending and I told her that I expected to be working at least two years longer in London before moving my practice to Sussex. This did not bring the relief I expected. At the end of a session in which she seemed very old and repetitive – and in which it was I who took on the burden of her ageing, not unmixed with my own – she started again when half out of the door – 'what I really wanted to say…' I said wearily, 'We've talked about it.' She said firmly that we hadn't. What she really wanted to say was that she realized she had to stop before she became physically incapable of coming. She thus repeated, and made her own, what I had said a year earlier. By my weakening and offering her more time, she was able to see that continuing for another two years would be unrealistic. I was relieved that, in this session, she made the decision herself and that I was not forcing on her a 'termination'.

As summer drew near, she was able to admit to some disappointment. She had hoped that I would cure her panic attacks. I invited her to air a bit of healthy disillusion, but she found this hard and murmured something about being teased for turning all her geese into swans. 'Does that make you a goose?' I said, and tried to show her that, by making me a swan, she depleted herself, and that, in that gap between us, there might be a hidden envy, anger, even hate. But she was determined to keep me above reproach.

The countdown was painful. When the time came for our last session, she took refuge in confusion. We were both going away on holiday. She said we should get out our diaries and arrange to meet again, but she found, to her dismay, that she had forgotten to bring her diary with her. I admitted, quite truthfully, that so had I, and that, by a curious chance, this was the only time I had ever forgotten to bring it to London. But, as I went on to explain, we had no need of diaries. 'What do you mean?' I said I thought she knew what I meant. After an awkward pause, she admitted that she knew quite well, 'But I'm wriggling.' Then she said again that, as long as she had me, she could postpone her old age. She left the room abruptly, murmuring that she did not want a 'grand finale'. I was sure that she was on the verge of tears and determined not to cry. Perhaps tears had been forbidden by her mother, whom I could imagine saying, 'You're a big girl now.'

We had a sort of finale that evening on the telephone. She had control of the situation and could ring off in her own time. She said what a horrid, rude, old woman she had been not to thank me for changing her life.

I had already promised to come one day and see her studio and all those paintings that were such an important part of her world. I said again that I looked forward to doing so, but only after a gap.

Looking back on our years together, I have mixed feelings. Whereas I am glad to have helped her through some critical times, I am also aware of what was avoided – death and hate. She had been left with work to do on herself and which, if she had the courage, she could only do *by* herself. The transference had not been neatly resolved and I was still a 'swan'. This was not comfortable for me, however much my narcissism was fed by her declaration that I had changed her life. That life continues to change and I am still there, on the fringe of it, and I suspect that this will continue until 'death us do part'.

We had our gap and, after I visited her studio, she managed for a year or so without further contact. As long as she was still painting, she saw some point in going on. Painting gave her the same sort of meaningfulness that she was sometimes sad not to have found in religion.

I think, on the whole, I am right in assuming that there is not much therapist/patient contact after the end of therapy and especially if that contact is not confined to the consulting room. My impression is that most of us, in the last session, assure our patients that the 'door is open', should they need to come back, even though they will have to risk waiting for a vacancy. Or we may decide to meet again in a few months time on a one-off basis to make sure that the patient is coping with post-therapy living. Most patients are grateful for an offer of this kind, but, in my experience, not many make use of it. In a recent goodbye, a patient, who had an anxious dream about ending (which she saw as a slippery slope and me as a beautiful animal that she had pushed down a ravine and killed), actually said to me on the doorstep that she hoped we would *not* meet again. She was just under 50 and, despite difficulties, still had opportunities in her external world for new beginnings. With much older patients, such beginnings will, most likely, be internal, although there may be hard choices ahead to do with losing independence through moving from an autonomous to a communal existence.

A lot is written about the need to mourn the therapist, as though this is the same as mourning yet another death. I think we should remember that when a loved person dies, be it spouse, parent or friend, that person is not going to belong to anyone else and that, as an internalized goodness, the love given to the mourner cannot be contaminated. The pattern is complete. The therapist, however, is not retiring from this world, not even from the consulting room; but the patient ending therapy can be pretty sure that another patient will soon be occupying his or her precious slot and that a whole crowd of other patients (seen as rivals) will be diverting the therapist's attention. There is often a fear of not being remembered, of not making a permanent impact on the therapist's consciousness. One may even imagine case notes being burned or, worse still, the destruction of poems and paintings. It may seem more like one's own death than the death of the therapist. And, in the countertransference, we, as therapists, may feel that we have killed our patients, which is one of the reasons for hoping that, in each case, the ending was the patient's free choice. I had to keep reminding myself, in the case described above, that although the old lady kept forgetting our decision and behaved as though it were I who imposed on her an unwelcome ending, there had been a time, just once, when I had offered more and she had refused my offer.

No wonder we often feel cruel, for we are insisting on a therapeutic death which we have probably managed to avoid ourselves. I was glad to find comments from various writers about this matter:

If it is maintained that termination *is* the right word, and that ending should be final complete and abrupt, then are we not asking patients to face something that we as analysts may never, or seldom, have to face? After qualification, a new analyst may continue to meet their therapist at professional meetings… (Pedder 1988, p.500)

They have the opportunity to see their analysts in the frame of reality, and the magic omnipotent features of the relationship collapse more rapidly under these conditions and may be replaced by a mature friendship or a working relationship. (Reich 1950, p.501)

I am sure it is true that getting to know the analyst or therapist in a less artificial setting is the easiest way to resolve the transference and bring about a necessary disillusion, through which a former patient can become aware that there will never be just one omnipotent saviour but a variety of helpers and friends, who come and go and inevitably fail at times. Malan, writing about endings, quotes Winnicott, who, whether referring to mothers or analysts, believed in the necessity of disillusion. He went so far as to say that 'the function of the therapist is not to succeed but to fail.'

Where a major part of the patient's problem consists of loss, deprivation and unfulfilled love, it is the therapist's task not to try and make this up to the patient – which is impossible – but to enable him to experience his true feelings about it and come out the other side. (Malan 1979, p.193)

But the carefully arranged end is not always the true end. Reading several accounts of an internalized therapy continuing long after the last session has set me thinking about whether sometimes, particularly with the really old, we may get the timing wrong. Marion Milner, writing about a younger age group, describes

what no longer coming to analysis meant to one particular patient. This ending was not something which happened as a logical result of the patient's being considered cured; in fact the ending preceded the cure by many months, for it was not until the analysis had actually stopped that the symptom began to move at all… It was not until the patient had felt that I had been really bad to her, by 'chucking her out', and at the same time I had taken responsibility for it, that she had…become free enough to begin life as a separate person with standards of her own. (Milner 1949, pp.73, 76)

When my patient at last let herself be 'chucked out', it seemed that she could only face age and death when she no longer had me there to cushion her. I have described how difficult it was to make an end and how much I had wanted it to be her choice rather than mine. On the other hand, I waited until her memory loss was impeding our progress. With hindsight, I can see that she might have been better able to work on her fears by herself if we had managed to end a year earlier. In much the same way, but some time later, the decision to go into residential care may have been left a year too late, for, although appreciating the beauty of her surroundings and the genuine concern of staff and helpers, the crucial question now had to be faced as to whether she could cope creatively with this upheaval so late in life and, if not, what alternative could be offered. She was able to enjoy the garden, flowers and trees. She had her easel and her paints, but she never managed to use them.

When I visited her within two days of her arrival, the future was doubtful. She was disorientated and confused, but, in between repetitions, we found ourselves talking about death. She had wanted to know what influence my work had on religious faith and I answered her as clearly as I could. She then surprised me – 'Everyone has to believe something.' I just asked, 'Do *you*?' Her answer was, 'Oh yes.' We said no more but I did not have that feeling of avoidance that I used to have in our therapy sessions. At the same time, I felt that she neither wanted, nor was able to voice, whatever ultimate concerns she had been quietly mulling over during the five years since our official ending. I had to respect that there had been something 'going on', whether or not either of us had consciously recognized it.

One of her last pictures during our therapy was stark, black and white and abstract, but it had, as its underlying theme, the myth of Apollo and Daphne and how Daphne was turned into a tree by Zeus to save her from rape. The story is almost lost in a pattern of fragmented shapes which, none the less, achieve balance and harmony. Something, or someone, is being wrenched apart, yet seems to be struggling towards the sun. Looking at it together, neither of us made any attempt at interpretation, but I think she knew she was communicating something and this was the only way it could be expressed. However savage, it was a picture about transformation.

I have often felt that in composing, and in appreciating, a work of art, an unconscious communication goes on between the artist and the one who perceives the finished artefact; and I am sure that something of this sort was happening when I looked at my patient's picture. Sometimes a critic seems to read more into a work than its composer consciously intended, in which case we might infer that their two unconsciousnesses touched in a process of projective identification; or that such communication is only possible if we posit a collective unconscious.

Jung tended to allow his older patients to pursue, when possible, their quests for individuation on their own, just as he had done himself, only coming to him when their dreams or fantasies needed elucidation. It is true that some ageing people become less personally involved in relationships, more inward-looking, sometimes detached from everyday concerns, but there are others who feel isolated and in need of continuing, though unobtrusive, support. My patient was one of these.

To achieve peace of mind, Jung advised us:

> If we can live in such a way that conscious and unconscious demands are taken into account as far as possible, then the centre of gravity of the total personality shifts its position. It is then no longer in the ego, which is merely the centre of consciousness, but in the hypothetical point between conscious and unconscious. This new centre might be called the Self. (Jung 1954, p.334)

This move from conscious to unconscious, from ego to Self, is the work of individuation. Some never achieve it and none of us do so completely; but perhaps, for most of us, it is possible at least some of the time. And I would like to add (though how can I know?) even in dementia.

My elderly patient is still alive but, after a fall and a broken hip, has moved to a nursing home and is reported by those who care for her to be dementing. I prefer to describe her (as I have already in the last chapter) as spending most of her time in an inner rather than an outer world.

Finally, I want to mention an ending between a counsellor and her client. This client, in her nineties, had a terror of death as extinction. She regarded faith as a gift that had not been given to her. The counsellor had formerly nursed in a hospice and absorbed the philosophy of living well in order to die well, within the context of close relationships. She asked herself whether all she was really doing was giving the same support which anyone else might have given; yet she was aware of a personal tie and that it was *her* presence that was needed. After two years, there came a time when her client was less afraid and ready to say goodbye. A last session was arranged but never happened. The old lady had died peacefully a few days before. Whatever the counsellor's faith did for her client's lack of it, some mysterious transformation seems to have taken place and the ending was perfectly timed.

I have sometimes noticed that counsellors are less hesitant than their tutors when it comes to taking on much older people. Perhaps innocence pays off. Not having read so much of the literature and perhaps not having such strict models which they feel they should follow, they are better able to trust their own instincts and insights. I hope they may continue with this non-ageist approach without too many supervisory misgivings getting in the way.

If individuation is the goal, as also the process, of therapy, we may hope that the end of life will not be overshadowed by terror of death. For as long as our egos are strong, there is likely to be a fear of losing that strength. Between the opposites of separation and fusion, death will be warded off or welcomed according to which way the pendulum swings at different times in a person's life. At the very end, when the ego does not so much weaken as surrender to the self; when the outside world becomes less inviting as well as less familiar, there is often a gradual detachment from emotional ties, achievements, relationships – and then, at last, death may be looked forward to as the end of separation and bringer of comfort. Sometimes there is a longing to be set free from the ravages of time and a wish for a timeless, and therefore unconscious, state of being. Rosemary Gordon, who has looked at some depth into dying and into creativity, has this to say:

> The perception of linear time is undoubtedly an ego function; it grows and develops in childhood, is reduced in senility, and is liable to distortion in psychotic conditions. Without the apprehension of linear time, there can be no conception of an end…the cosmic experience of time is symbolized by the circle – the circle that has no beginning and no end – for each point on it is both beginning and end. (Gordon 1993, pp.116–117)

It is strange that we talk of the life *cycle* but continue to see it as a straight line from cradle to grave. Only artists and mystics – perhaps my old patient in her senility, and those near to death – can enter into a truly cosmic experience. Yet before we reach this state, we need to move, to grow, to change and not to cling. The dying person's surrender is at best not a frightened or resentful resignation but a courageous openness to transformation and not knowing. As patients, as therapists, and as human beings, we may hope for some of that openness before our body's death, and to have also that essential 'negative capability' – mentioned by Keats in a letter to his brother and now, surprisingly, a catch-phrase among therapists – which makes it possible not to know, and not to worry about not knowing, the ultimate answers to our human condition.

CHAPTER 12

The Ageing Therapist

So far, I have written about ageing patients and their suitability for therapy. I have criticized ageist attitudes. In looking at the lengthening lives of older people today, I have rejected any form of stereotyping that places newly retired – or not yet retired – 60-year-olds in the same category as those in their nineties, without taking into account the generation gap between them. I have advocated using the terms 'young old' and 'old old' to describe this difference, although I am aware that such grouping may bring about further stereotyping if we fail to notice what a variety of individuals there are within these groups, and how manifold their ways and rates of ageing.

In writing about the role of the therapist, I have stressed the need for respect, for an open mind and a sense of history. It would seem that those I had in mind were young or middle-aged working with patients older than themselves. But, as I have already mentioned, ours is not a profession in which early retirement is the norm and there are quite a number of therapists, well into their sixties, seventies and even eighties, who have most probably given up institutional work but are still in private practice and working with a variety of age groups.

Speaking for myself, I tend these days to refer any very young patients who come my way to younger colleagues. Patients in their thirties may be happy with me as a mother figure but I am doubtful about grandparenting teenagers, some of whom speak a language that, to me, is strange and new. I have kept up with 'fab' and 'brill' but not with words like 'wicked' meaning 'good'. And, if I were to take the trouble to learn these words, the result, I am sure, would sound artificial and even pathetic.

Earlier in this book, I mentioned an adolescent who thought I had been alive in Victoria's reign, and how I retorted (I think now rather arrogantly, and, of course defensively) that she knew nothing of age but I understood about being young because I had 'been there'. I realize now that, although, in youth, I had lived through the same universal phases of human development and been gripped by the same archetypes (though perhaps with different images), I had not actually inhabited the same space, the same time and exactly the same culture as one who grew up in the century's later years. In fact, we never do replicate another person's experience, and it goes without saying that 'I know just how you feel' is not only no help but untrue.

We need therefore to recognize that our own life-experience is irrelevant but not useless. It can be used in that it affects our countertransference and we need perhaps to throw out what belongs only to our personal history at a particular time and place, while, at the same time, allowing ourselves to react emotionally so that we can enter imaginatively into the other person's context, which is not quite ours and yet not quite separate from whatever circumstances we have lived through and remember. We need to acknowledge difference as well as identification, and to risk those meeting-points which transect rather than run parallel to another experience. Bion's advice – 'Discard your memory; discard the future tense of your desire' (Bion 1967, pp.271–280) applies to therapists of all ages, but perhaps growing older on the job facilitates the mix of detachment and close attention which he advocates. A voluntary discarding of memory in order to make room for a new idea is, of course, what is meant, and a concentration on the reality of the present moment rather than what *we* want, and what *we* hope the patient will turn into, after therapy. Older therapists have shorter futures and fewer desires that they can realistically expect to be fulfilled. This may make for greater wisdom. On the other hand, it may not, in which case it could be time (high time) to retire.

There are certain questions I need to keep asking myself. I have always been proud of my memory. Is its gradual diminishment getting in the way of good work, or does it leave my mind less cluttered and more open to take Bion's advice? I only know that I lose pieces of paper and forget where I put things. Now and then, I forget names. But I still remember what interests me most and my range of interests seems to be wider rather than more limited as I get older.

Hearing may become a problem. There has been deafness in my family and also denial of deafness. My patients seem to mumble more these days – or perhaps not. But I am not asking for a hearing aid yet. A new patient complained of my ticking clock. I was surprised and replied truthfully that I never hear it. Other people tell me that it is audible but no louder than average. I plan to retire before deafness becomes a major problem.

Although the therapist, in the transference, can be experienced timelessly and the erotic discovered in unlikely places, one of my male patients admitted that he had been disappointed since the beginning that I was too old to be the object of his sexual fantasies. He reminded me of the first dream he ever reported in which I was an aloof figure in a churchyard and he was making love to my daughter. Another patient, some years older, dreamed of sex with me culminating in a huge orgasm in which I was both his lover and his mother giving him birth. He seemed to be offering this dream as a gift and I accepted it warmly.

In an American book, *How Psychiatrists look at Ageing*, Bernard Bandler writes, 'Retirement is a dress rehearsal for death,' a statement that could hardly be more stark! He looks at earlier losses, all of them followed by restitution: 'Growth is the mastery of loss...the sorrow of separation is submerged in the joy of anticipation.' But the final goodbye to work comes at a time when there is less to anticipate. 'Testimonials and honours are a form of farewell' (Bandler 1992, p.42). Yet he goes on to write about all sorts of new interests and the rediscovery, even while his body was running downhill, of 'the sense of wonder and mystery of childhood...there is no compulsion that the spirit, barring irreparable damage to the brain, should follow the seasons of the body and embrace winter' (Ibid., p.44).

Another writer, Mervin Hurwitz, contributing to the same book, states: 'My impression after living and working with analysts for decades is that very few retire. Some decrease their working time somewhat and call that retirement, but complete retirement is rare. I think that most die in harness' (Hurwitz 1992, p.97). He describes how an analyst of his acquaintance worked until a week before his death from cancer, allowing his patients to watch him slowly fade away. This was an extreme case but he does not think it unique – in fact I have heard of others. Such dedicated behaviour has to do with the analyst's concern for patients and their fear of separation, but perhaps just as much with the analyst's own fears and anxieties, as though continuing work could postpone the impact of these feelings.

Hurwitz, himself, had made no plans for retirement, but thought of himself as going on for ever with improved rather than diminishing abilities. As he approached 60, a series of mishaps, due to osteo-arthritis, cancer and coronary occlusion, brought him up against his mortality. Going back to work, he struggled with his narcissism, guilt and anger, and so wore himself out that he had to face the inevitable and settle on a date to finish with his patients. He chose the end of July and thereby gave himself an extra month (which would have been his summer break) to go on denying that his career was over. The trauma of this decision brought on congestive heart failure, which luckily was mild enough to clear up with treatment. Looking back, he feels that he would have been helped if he had gone back into analysis when he had to face retirement. I am reminded of Fordham's analysis with Meltzer, at the age of 79. But, as far as I know, Fordham, who lived to be nearly 90, never formally retired.

I wonder how many analysts and psychotherapists have actually taken Hurwitz's advice or followed Fordham's example and who, among younger colleagues, would be prepared to engage in such an enterprise with those whom they have come to regard as seniors and teachers. One would admire both the humility of the older and the courage of younger therapists were they to do so.

In envisaging such an eventuality, I feel that we are exploring the nub of what this book is about – that, whatever age we are and whichever side we are on in the therapist/patient partnership, it is not, in Tennyson's words, 'too late to seek a newer world'. And our task might be (as in the last line of the same poem, 'Ulysses') 'to strive, to seek, to find and not to yield.'

Pre-retirement courses are on offer these days, both in industry and in some of the professions. I heard of one being held at a United Nations Centre, in which, after practical advice about pensions, there was a seminar on personal adjustment. This was taken by a Jungian analyst, presumably one who was still in full-time work. What help, I wondered, would this analyst be given when his turn came round to retire. Perhaps this is a subject to which psychotherapeutic societies and institutions should give some thought.

Thinking about retirement – and my impression is that a lot of us think about it even as we postpone doing it – I wrote to two of my colleagues, one who had already retired and another who was on the point of doing so. Both found that the experience was traumatic and difficult to talk about. Both mentioned separation anxiety. The colleague who has gone through the process was already seeing fewer patients and thinking about retirement when she had a serious accident. This acted as a trigger towards setting a definite retirement date. Colleagues commented very little though several expressed surprise and a few close friends said they felt envious of her capacity to act decisively. She writes: 'I suppose people vary in the extent to which their identity is tied up in their work. I'm sure, however, that I can't be too unusual in discovering that the whole business of being a therapist was central to my being…the balance of my psychic equilibrium was upset when I gave up that role.'

Other colleagues, still working, say that, in the absence of an adequate pension, they need the money. Those who live alone would miss the continuous coming and going of patients, the intense involvement in their different lives and being an all-important figure for so many people.

Our society is inclined, I think, to equate who we are with what we do, and, most especially with a professional doing, by which we earn our money. If retired, we may find ourselves introduced as someone who *was* a psychotherapist, as if we once had an identity which has now gone missing. To fill this hole, we may throw ourselves immediately into new commitments. There may be all sorts of interests that we never had time to pursue, and, at last, a golden opportunity awaits us. But I would like to think that some of us could manage to do nothing – at least some of the time – and just be. If so, retirement is indeed a dress rehearsal, not only for death but for a private being and doing, with an emphasis on being, which is another, and perhaps fuller, mode of existence than a lot of bustling activity. In 'old old' age, we may have to learn that receiving is sometimes more blessed than giving, and to be gracious in saying thank you to those who generously (or even grudgingly) give to us.

I am still 'thinking about' retirement and I see it as a gradual letting go, a decision not to take on new patients and to come to an end with the others in each one's appropriate time. When this is done, I should like to feel that psychotherapy is what I have done with an important part of my life but not the whole of it.

CHAPTER 13

Matters of Life and Death

A recent conversation with a colleague went something like this:

SHE: You really seem to believe in what you are doing. Don't you
ever have doubts?

ME: Of course. All the time.

SHE: Then – why do you do it?

ME: Why do *you*?

SHE: In the hope that one day I'll get it right. But I keep feeling – both
in my own analysis and in what I give to others – something's
lacking.

ME: But – you can't expect perfection.

SHE: If not, what's the point?

ME: *(after floundering a bit)* Healthy disillusion.

Sometimes I think I invented this phrase, and perhaps I did, even though, as
we have already seen, others have used it before me.

There is a stage in growing up that, I think, applies both to psychotherapy
and to the wider arena of life, during which one expects solutions and assumes
that special people exist – parents, teachers, therapists – who are mysteriously
'in the know' and can guide us along one exactly right path to arrive at exactly
the right place. Fundamentalists, whether Christian or Moslem, when they seek
salvation, expect this illusory perfection. Arguably, it is a necessary part of being
young (children need strong boundaries), or applies as much to the very old,
whose childlike trust in God, or whatever their mothers taught them, must
never be shaken – though I question this assumption.

In my chapter on endings, I described one that was long-drawn-out and far
from perfect. In fact it might be considered messy enough to serve as a warning

against long-term work with old people! However, I have some faith that the therapy was good enough while it lasted. The healthy disillusion was mine rather than the patient's and perhaps saves me from inflation.

As for my colleague's question about doubt, I have just answered it in using the word faith; for here is another of those paradoxes which keep playing tricks on us. As a pair of opposites, faith and doubt need each other. If there were no doubt, faith would not be faith but knowledge, and, without faith, those who doubt might tumble into despair. It is not the job of the therapist to know but to be able to get along with uncertainty and perhaps help others to recognize that Keats' 'negative capability' is an essential asset. Since we do not claim to know, and therefore to expect a specific outcome (or cure), we are free to hope that all those long hours of being together may, in some way or other, bring surprises. It would be foolish to wish for gratitude but we most of us prefer love to hate, and, as I have already shown, I am not able to dismiss all loving feelings as belonging only to the transference. Having talked of faith and hope, it seems natural to add love, even while acknowledging a mixture of hate – likewise not always transferential. Illusions fall away, suddenly or gradually, and the other person's reality emerges, with all its blemishes, into a daylight unenhanced with any rosy glow. That is the best we are likely to experience, which is probably healthier than being plunged into a wholly negative darkness.

What is often sad for the therapist is not knowing the end of a person's story and this, if our patients are old, may mean missing their dying. Even if given the chance to attend a funeral or memorial service, the anonymous therapist tactfully sits at the back while the relatives go through their rituals of mourning. On one such occasion, I listened to a sermon about the deceased and hardly recognized him as my patient. It was not that I disbelieved what I heard but I felt privileged to have known the private person behind his public persona.

Only twice have I seen patients who were known to be terminally ill. Both were girls in their twenties. The first persisted in denying that death was inevitable and beseeched me to assure her that she would be cured by positive thinking. All I could say – and keep repeating – was 'I don't know.' She left me for a guru who promised a cure. The other was realistic but became too ill too quickly for us to continue. I got no more than a glimpse of that speeding up of what most of us can postpone or work through at a slower pace, the task of accepting our mortality. Keats, at an early age, declared in 'Ode to a Nightingale' that he had 'been half in love with easeful death'. He too was terminally ill and had to accelerate his ageing. He must sometimes have longed just to end his suffering.

Unless bereaved or as ill as the two I have mentioned, our younger patients are usually more concerned with life than death. With middle age comes an awareness of limitation and perhaps regrets about missed chances and mourning for potentialities never to be realized. The fact of death gives life a shape and one may even anticipate its final pattern. but sometimes the meaning gets lost. 'I'm just waiting for my pension,' says a woman of 50, 'And after that, there's a blank.' Ten years later, she retires and waits for death, and that is a final blank, sometimes frightening and sometimes cosy, 'Like being tucked up in bed at night'. She says that she would like to die with a crowd of people, in a shipwreck or an air crash. Then her mood changes and she murmurs desolately, 'We're all alone in the end.'

But how alone are we? Jung saw our seemingly separate identities as part of a collective psyche. He gave us the image of islands emerging from the sea. On the level of the sea-bed, all the land was joined. Sometimes we are aware of a symbiotic merging, both in infancy and on the analytic couch. Nathan Field, writing about projective identification as communication, and also about the paranormal, has this to say:

> I am arguing therefore not simply that we enter into states of merger, but that we already exist in a state of merger. From the viewpoint of consciousness we appear separate individuals with a regrettable tendency to lapse into fantasies of fusion; but if we look through the other end of the telescope we will see that the fact of our connection is primary and that our sense of separateness is sustained by a system of defences that differentiates us one from another. This is not to diminish human individuality but to emphasize how fragile it is, and how vigilantly we must protect it. We must ask if this collective psyche applies only to the human unconscious, or could we envisage some vast ocean of unconsciousness which we share with all living creatures and beyond that with an infinite continuum that underlies existence itself. (Field 1991, pp.97–8)

He also quotes Jung as bringing physics and psychology together: 'Since psyche and matter are contained in one and the same world and moreover are in continuous contact with one another and ultimately rest on irrepresentable transcendental factors, it is not only possible but fairly probable even, that psyche and matter are two aspects of the same thing' (Jung 1983, p.130).

What Field describes as living in a fourth dimension occurs in out-of-the-body experiences, in meditation, in our dreams and sometimes, I think, in bereavement. I wonder also whether it is present in some of the disoriented states of extreme old age. In order to accept the end of the only life we know, we may have to let go of vigilance and allow ourselves to be fragile. Individuation, which we must remember, is a process, not a state, may at the end become a gathering up of all the odds and ends of our personal experience in order to affect and enrich the whole of existence.

This would be pure speculation if we did not have so many records of the heightened consciousness experienced by those individuals who have found themselves right at the edge of what we like to think of as normal human life. One such record is by Jung himself:

> It seemed to me that I was high up in space. Far below I saw the globe of the earth, bathed in a gloriously blue light…I knew that I was at the point of departing from the earth… Something new entered my field of vision…I saw in space a tremendous dark block of stone… It was floating in space and I was floating in space…I had the feeling that everything was being sloughed away; everything I aimed or wished for or thought, the whole phantasmagoria of earthly existence, fell away or was stripped from me – an extremely painful process. Nevertheless something remained; it was as if I now carried along with me everything I had ever experienced or done, everything that had happened around me. I might also say: it was with me and I was it…I consisted of my own history, and I felt with great certainty: this is what I am. 'I am this bundle of what has been, and what has been accomplished.' (Jung 1963, pp.320–321)

This passage is much abbreviated but can be found in full in Jung's autobiography, *Memories, Dreams, Reflections.*

Stanislav Grof, who helped his patients with psychedelic drugs in order to ease the experience of dying from cancer, describes somewhat similar states.

> I was alone in a timeless world with no boundaries. There was no atmosphere; there was no colour, no imagery, but there may have been light. Suddenly I recognized that I was a moment in time, created by those before me and in turn the creator of others. This was my moment and my major function had been completed. (p.23)

And another voice: 'There is a lot to me, much more than I ever suspected; there are forms, colours and textures – indescribable…' (Grof and Halifax 1977, pp.99).

We often hear from people who have near-fatal accidents and an experience of dying which they remember when resuscitated. They feel disembodied and, as they move from darkness to light, can make a life-review. Often they do not want to be revived and, according to most reports, they lose all fear of death.

If, during our so-called ordinary life, we were able, as Field suggests, to look through the other end of the telescope, we might perhaps acknowledge more of this dimension than we usually realize. In our dreams, we inhabit a different space-time and sometimes converse with the dead. It is not unusual to dream of a person on the night of his death, although most of these dreams are never reported or written down, leaving us without any indisputable evidence that they occurred. We may have conversations of great meaning to our dreaming selves but wake repeating inconsequential sentences that remind us of psychotic or demented speech. Instead of laughing away this 'nonsense', it might be helpful if we tried interpreting the language of those who live continuously in dreams. I have given an example in an earlier book of conversing with an Alzheimer's patient:

> ...she pounded the side of her chair and screamed at him, [sic] 'who's taking care of that baby?' He sat down and tried to work out what she was trying to say. Which baby? He thought of blaming the television and the soap opera going on in front of her... But the baby was not on television. On the far side of the room, another old lady, also chairbound, was screaming for her mother and no one was responding. So I spoke to Harriet about her mothering, her own sense of the importance of children... She calmed down...I suggested to Harriet that perhaps I should go over and help the child crying for her mother... (Butler and Orbach 1993, p.152)

The old lady's visitor (not a trained analyst but a priest) commented:

> We live in a very rational world – people want to know what time it is – they want to know where they are going next – all those things that you and I worry about. I often feel that with the confused you can chat heart to heart. You can touch people where we really come together. (Ibid.)

There is a special fragility in the newly bereaved which seems at times to make the usual conscious/unconscious barriers permeable. Their experiences have been described, rather dismissively, as hallucinations and this is, I suppose, accurate in that the dead are no longer materially present. Some people describe both seeing and hearing. Others cannot translate the experience into a language of human sensation, though I have a report by one who tried: 'I didn't see him, nor did he speak, though I cried out to him; nor did I feel his actual touch – but it was more like touching than anything else. What I felt was very intense, blissful, but almost more than I could bear.'

Being able to live with an extra dimension is compared by Field with the shift that had to be made from a flat to a spherical image of the earth, and how hard that had been to accept. I remember this non-acceptance, when, at the age of six, I looked at the sea's horizon which seemed to me to have a very sharp edge which one could surely fall off.

'Out of the mouths of babes' comes a common-sense view of death. A five-year-old, standing in a crowded place, was obviously doing some hard thinking. At last she turned to me and said, 'I know why people have to die. It's because more babies keep being born, and if we all stayed alive, there wouldn't be room.' Earlier in this book, I touched on the theme of serenity and came to no definite conclusion; nor do I now; but, if the very old could really accept such a dictum and move graciously out of the way of their descendants – that indeed would be serenity! But I find myself wondering – will that little girl, when her turn comes, be ready to move on?

There can be no perfect end, neither to life nor to this book. Both as therapists and as patients, we are left with enormous questions. What is consciousness? What is the meaning of life? What is death? We have no facts but plenty of symbols, and we may even find that the old and demented are capable of symbolic communication – if only we will take the trouble to listen and attend to what they say. That, in itself, is therapy and has to do with the root meaning of the word – θεραπεια – attendance.

Postscript

The night after finishing my last chapter, I had a dream which was both vivid and elusive. Waking in the middle, I thought it so memorable that this dream at least would not be lost. The next day was a mixture of sun and shadow and it was late afternoon before the clouds lifted at last, and it was then that my dream came back to me as though from a long way off. I also remembered hearing on the news that there had been a possibility that night of seeing meteorites shooting through the sky at the rate of one a second. But I had forgotten to look. The dream was full of menace. 'We' were on an open plain being pursued by something indescribable – something beautiful, transparent and alien. There seemed no escape from being surrounded, entangled and shot through. If the unknown 'thing' got inside us, we were sure to be destroyed. For a moment I was awake enough to know it was a dream and that I had a choice of whether to get up and shake it off or to go on with it and face the danger. I sank back into the dream but, this time, I said to myself, 'The "thing" can't get at me if I ignore it. If I'm not afraid, it might go away.' The 'thing' became more distant but remained on the horizon and I fell into a deep sleep.

No wonder I forgot and only retain a shadowy picture of something too alien to describe. Who were 'we'? Perhaps I identified with all frightened humans confronted, as we have to be, with the unknown. As for ignoring this alien 'thing' in order to save our sanity, that is what we have to do most of the time. Human kind, wrote Eliot in 'Burnt Norton', 'Cannot bear very much reality.' At least in my dream the 'thing' was beautiful, even though taking it into myself would destroy me. And yet by 'me', all I can possibly mean is my ego. And when I say 'we', perhaps I am realizing how much more there is, with which my 'me' can be joined.

In the face of ageing and death, there are no certainties, but many different experiences. Those who go on hoping, as they have done all their lives, for a meaningful climax, must be those whose infancy was comfortable and secure enough to engender lasting hopefulness and trust. Those who began life without that kind of love, and therefore without that basic hope and trust, are not so likely to grasp these helpful lifebuoys as they move into old age. As therapists, we must realize that such feelings cannot be magically given by us, but any optimism or acceptance that we can manage to have ourselves may perhaps be infectious enough to carry them some of the way, so that, as in my dream, they can see beauty as well as terror; and that death need not be a meaningless escape from a life without hope, but a natural metamorphosis.

To quote a lifelong agnostic: 'I'm ready to fit in with the arrangements, whatever they turn out to be.'

References

Abraham, G., Kocher, P. and Goda, G. (1980) 'Psychoanalysis and ageing.' *International Review of Psychoanalysis*, 147–155.

Abraham, K. (1948) *The Applicability of Psychoanalytic Treatment to Patients of an Advanced Age*. Selected Edition. London: Hogarth Press.

Adler, G. (1979) *The Dynamics of the Self*. London: Coventure Ltd.

Balint, M. (1933) 'Problems of growing old.' From *Problems of Human Pleasure and Behaviour*, reprinted in 1987. London: Maresfield Library.

Balint, M. (1968) *The Basic Fault*. London: Routledge.

Bandler, B. (1992) 'The ageing process.' From *How Psychiatrists Look at Ageing* (Mental Health Library Series, Monograph 1). G.H. Pollock (ed). Madison, CT: International University Press.

Bellack, L. and Small, L. (1965) *Emergency Psychotherapy and Brief Psychotherapy*. New York: Grune and Stratton.

Bettelheim, B. (1985) *Freud and Man's Soul*. London: Flamingo.

Bion, W.R. (1967) 'Notes on memory and desire.' *Psychoanalytic Forum 2*, 271–80.

Bollas, C. (1986) 'The transformational object.' From *The British School of Psychoanalysis, The Independent Movement*. G. Kohon (ed) London: Free Association Books.

Bollas, C. (1987) *The Shadow of the Object: The Psychoanalysis of the Unthought Thought*. London: Free Association Books.

Boswell, J. (1791) *The Life of Doctor Johnson*. London: Methuen, 1991.

Brewer, E.C. (1959) 'Dying sayings.' From *Brewer's Dictionary of Phrase and Fable*. London: Cassel and Co.

Bunyan, J. (1678) *The Pilgrim's Progress*. Cambridge: Heffer and Sons, 1939.

Butler, M. and Orbach, A. (1993) *Being Your Age*. London: SPCK, New Library of Pastoral Care.

Butler, R.N. (1963) 'The life review: an interpretation of reminiscence in the aged.' *Psychiatry 26*, February, 65–76.

Butler, R.N. (1975) 'The elderly: an overview.' *American Journal of Psychiatry 132*, 893–900.

Butler, R.N. (1978) 'The creative life of old age.' Quoted in *Group Therapy for the Elderly*, Monogram 5, American Group Psychotherapy Association, 219

Butler, R.N. and Lewis, M.I. (1974) *Ageing and Mental Health: Positive Psychosocial Approaches*. St. Louis: Mosby.

Cohen, G.D. (1985) 'Psychotherapy with an eighty-year-old patient.' In *The Race Against Time*. M.A. Nemiroff and A. Colarusso (eds) New York and London: Plenum Press.

Erikson, E. (1959) 'Identity and the life cycle.' *Psychological Issues*, Monograph 1, New York.

Erikson, E. (1981) 'Elements of a psychodynamic theory of social development.' In S.I. Greenspan and G.H. Pollock. *The Course of Life 6*, Washington: National Institute of Mental Health.

Etchegoyen, H. (1983) 'Fifty years after the mutative interpretation.' *International Journal of Psychoanalysis 64*, 445–459.

Farber, L. (1976) *The Ways of the Will*, now reprinted as *Lying, Despair, Jealousy, Envy, Sex, Suicide, Drugs and the Good Life*. Basic Books.

Field, N. (1991) 'Projective identification: mechanism or mystery?' *Journal of Analytical Psychology 36*, 93–109.

Fordham, M. (1978) *Jungian Psychotherapy*. Chichester: John Wiley and Sons Ltd.

Fordham, M. (1993) *The Making of an Analyst*. London: Free Association Books.

Freud, S. (1905) *On Psychotherapy*, Selected Edition. Vol.VII. London: Hogarth Press.

Freud, S. (1933) 'On femininity.' From *New Introductory Lectures*. London: Penguin, 1973.

Freud, S. and Breuer, J. (1974) *Studies in Hysteria*. London: Pelican.

Friedan, B. (1993) *The Fountain of Age*. London: Jonathan Cape.

von Goethe, J.W. (1987) *Faust Part Two*, trans. P. Wayne. Harmondsworth: Penguin.

Golding, W. (1955) *The Inheritors*. London: Faber and Faber Ltd.

Gordon, R. (1993) *Bridges, Metaphor for Psychic Processes*. London: Karnac Books Ltd.

Gould, R.L. (1985) *Transformations: Growth and Change in Adult Life*. New York: Simon and Schuster. Quoted in *The Race Against Time*. R.A. Nemiroff and C.A. Colarusso (eds). New York and London: Plenum Press.

Greenson, R. (1974) *The Technique and Practice of Psychoanalysis* Vol. 1. London: Hogarth Press.

Grof, S. and Halifax, J. (1977) *The Human Encounter with Death*. London: Souvenir Press Ltd.

Guggenbuhl-Craig, A. (1991) 'The old fool.' *Harvest 37*, Journal of the Analytical Psychology Club.

Herbert, G. (1934) 'The pulley.' From *The Oxford Book of Seventeenth Century Verse*. Oxford University Press.

Hildebrand, H.P. (1985) 'Object loss in the second half of life.' From *The Race Against Time*. R.A. Nemiroff and A. Colarusso (eds) New York and London: Plenum Press.

Hildebrand, H.P. (1982) 'Psychotherapy with older patients.' *British Journal of Medical Psychology*.

Hubback, J. (1988) *People Who Do Things To Each Other, Essays in Analytical Psychology*. Wilmet, III: Chiron Publications.

Hunter, J. (1986) 'Brief psychotherapy for unresolved grief, a clinical example from later life.' *British Journal of Psychotherapy 2*, 3, 186–195.

Hurwitz, M.H. (1992) 'The ageing process.' From *How Psychiatrists look at Ageing*. International University Press, inc. Mental Health Library Series, Monograph 1, G.H. Pollock (ed) Madison Connecticut.

Jones, E. (1957) *Sigmund Freud, Life and Work*, Vol.III. London: Hogarth Press.

Jung, C.G. (1929) *Commentary on the Secret of the Golden Flower*, Collected Works 13. London: Routledge and Kegan Paul.

Jung, C.G. (1946) *The Psychology of the Transference*. Collected Works 16, reprinted in Ark Paperbacks. London: Routledge and Kegan Paul 1983.

Jung, C.G. (1953) *Two Essays on Analytical Psychology.* Collected Works 7. London: Routledge and Kegan Paul.

Jung, C.G. (1954) *The Realities of Practical Psychotherapy.* Collected Works 6. London: Routledge and Kegan Paul 1981.

Jung, C.G. (1956) *Symbols of Transformation.* Collected Works 5, Bollingen Series. Princeton, NJ: Princeton University Press 1990.

Jung, C.G. (1963) *Memories, Dreams, Reflections.* London: Collins, Fontana Library.

Jung, C.G. (1983) *Selected Writings.* A. Storr (ed). London: Fontana Pocket Readers.

King, P. (1980) 'The life cycle as indicated by the nature of the transference in the psychoanalysis of the middle-aged and elderly.' *International Journal of Psychoanalysis 61*, 153–60.

Kohut, H. (1977) *The Restoration of the Self.* New York: N.Y. Universities Press.

Lacan, J. (1966) *Ecrits.* Quoted by B. Benvenuto and R. Kennedy in *The Works of Jacques Lacan* (1996). London: Free Association Books.

Lambert, K. (1981) *Analysis, Repair and Individuation.* London: Academic Press.

Laplanche, J. and Pontalis, J.B. (1973) *The Language of Psychoanalysis.* London: Hogarth Press.

Larkin, P. (1990) 'The old fools' and 'Aubade.' *Collected Poems.* London: Faber and Faber Ltd.

Lederman, R. (1991) 'Regression and stagnation.' *Journal of Analytical Psychology 61*, 483–504

Little, M.I. (1990) *Psychotic Anxieties and Containment, A Personal Record of Analysis with Winnicott.* Northvale, New Jersey and London: Jason Aaronson Inc.

Malan, D.H. (1979) *Individual Psychotherapy and the Science of Psychodynamics.* London: Butterworth.

Mann, T. (1971) *Death in Venice.* London: Penguin.

Marquez, G.G. (1989) *Love in the Time of Cholera.* London: Penguin.

Mehta, V. (1977) *Mahatma Gandhi and his Apostles.* London: André Deutsch Ltd.

Milner, M. (1949) 'The ending of two analyses.' In *The Suppressed Madness of Sane Men.* London: Routledge, 1988, 73–76.

Mitford, N. (1960) *Madame de Pompadour.* London: Penguin.

Montague, W. (1656) Quoted in *The Oxford English Dictionary,* (compact edition) Oxford University Press, 1979, 24720.

Nemiroff, R.A. and Colarusso, C.A. (1981) *Adult Development, A New Development in Psychodynamic Theory and Practice.* New York and London: Plenum Press, quoted in *The Race Against Time* (1985).

Nemiroff, R.A. and Colarusso, C.A. (eds) (1985) *The Race Against Time.* New York and London: Plenum Press.

Pedder, J. (1988) 'Termination reconsidered.' *International Journal of Psychoanalysis 69*, 495–505.

Plato (1908) *The Republic of Plato,* tr. J.L. Davies and D.J. Vaughan. London: Macmillan.

Pollock, G.H. (1988) 'The mourning liberation process: ideas on the inner life of the older adult.' From *Treating the Elderly with Psychotherapy.* J. Sadrov and M. Leszez (eds) Madison, Connecticut: International University Press, inc.

Rayner, E. (1990) *The Independent Mind in Psychoanalysis.* London: Free Association Books.

Reich, A. (1950) 'On the termination of analysis.' *International Journal of Psychoanalysis 31*, 179–83.

St Augustine (1945) *The Confessions*, Tr. F.J. Sheed. London: Sheed and Ward.

Strachey, I. (1934) 'The nature of the therapeutic action of psychoanalysis.' *International Journal of Psychoanalysis 15*, 127–159.

Winnicott, D.W. (1949) 'Mind and its relation to psyche-soma.' In *Through Paediatrics to Psychoanalysis*. London: Hogarth Press.

Winnicott, D.W. (1967) 'The location of cultural experience.' From *Playing and Reality*. London: Pelican, 1985.

Winnicott, D.W. (1974) 'Fear of breakdown.' *International Review of Psychoanalysis*, reprinted in *The British School of Psychoanalysis, The Independent Tradition*. G. Kohon (ed) London: Free Association Books.

Woolf, V. (1926) From *The Shorter Diaries of Virginia Woolf*, 27 February 1926. London: Hogarth Press.

Zoha, L. (1983) 'Working against Dorian Gray.' *Journal of Analytical Psychology 28*, 1, 51.

Index